The Time-Life Gardener's Guide

FOLIAGE HOUSEPLANTS

A
REDEFINITION
BOOK

Other Publications:

MYSTERIES OF THE UNKNOWN
TIME FRAME
FIX IT YOURSELF
FITNESS, HEALTH & NUTRITION
SUCCESSFUL PARENTING
HEALTHY HOME COOKING
UNDERSTANDING COMPUTERS
LIBRARY OF NATIONS
THE ENCHANTED WORLD
THE KODAK LIBRARY OF CREATIVE PHOTOGRAPHY
GREAT MEALS IN MINUTES
THE CIVIL WAR
PLANET EARTH
COLLECTOR'S LIBRARY OF THE CIVIL WAR
THE EPIC OF FLIGHT
THE GOOD COOK
WORLD WAR II
HOME REPAIR AND IMPROVEMENT
THE OLD WEST

For information on and a full description of any of
the Time-Life Books series listed above, please call 1-800-621-7026
or write:

Reader Information
Time-Life Customer Service
P.O. Box C-32068
Richmond, Virginia 23261-2068

This book is one of a series of guides to good gardening.

The Time-Life Gardener's Guide

FOLIAGE HOUSEPLANTS

TIME-LIFE BOOKS, ALEXANDRIA, VIRGINIA

CONTENTS

1
GREENING THE INDOORS

2
REJUVENATING AND REPLICATING

3
SHOWING OFF YOUR HOUSEPLANTS

Most foliage houseplants are tropical or semitropical in origin, hence their ability to survive the warm and more or less stable temperatures of indoor environments. Beyond that and the fact that they seldom flower, or flower only inconspicuously, they cover a broad range of botanical groupings, and of textures, forms and colors. Most are green, but some come in purples, reds and golds.

This volume will show you how to nurture, propagate and display foliage houseplants, whatever their origins and their habits. The first chapter explains soil preparation and potting techniques; the second, various means of propagation; the third, assorted ways of showing your plants to best advantage. Following those chapters is a section with a guide to seasonal maintenance, detailing some of the problems that beset houseplants, together with the causes of and solutions to those problems, and some handy tips. The volume concludes with an illustrated dictionary describing the genus and species of more than 125 of the exotic plants that can be grown for their foliage indoors.

4

MAKING THE MOST OF NATURE

5

DICTIONARY OF HOUSEPLANTS

1
GREENING THE INDOORS

Houseplants are wonderfully ingratiating. A geranium growing in a discarded coffee can has the same potential for pleasure as one growing in a porcelain cachepot. Both accommodate easily to their unfamiliar environment, provided that the environment comes reasonably close to the conditions the plant enjoyed in nature. And the same holds true for all houseplants—the cascading vines and stiff-leaved bromeliads, the spiky cacti and feathery ferns, the old favorites such as philodendron, rubber plant, snake plant and the ubiquitous Swedish ivy.

Alike in their ability to grow indoors, all of these houseplants nevertheless have distinctive preferences for soil, for light and shade, for nutrients, and for degrees of moisture around their roots and humidity around their foliage. For some, these preferences change with the plant's cycle of growth. Depending on season and on whether the plant is actively growing, it may require more or less sunlight or shade, more or less watering, and periodic booster shots of nutrients.

The instructions on the following pages are designed to simplify this care. They explain, for example, when and how to water, including even a clever watering system that works like the wick of an oil lamp, pulling a continuous supply of water from a reservoir through a length of cotton cord. An ideal solution for moisture-loving plants, wick watering also takes care of the problem of watering plants when their owners are away from home. Other instructions deal with potting and repotting, with the common problem of providing humidity—especially during the winter months, when central heating dries out the indoor air—and with pinching and pruning to keep mature plants tidy and well groomed. The section begins with a discussion of soils, the first order of business.

REPOTTING AN ESTABLISHED PLANT IN A NEW CONTAINER

Well-tended houseplants can grow with surprising speed and therefore need to be replanted in larger pots when they outgrow their old ones. Fortunately for the indoor gardener, a plant that has become pot-bound usually gives off clear signals of distress. The roots may start poking out of the drainage hole in the bottom of the pot, or they may grow upward, becoming visible on the surface of the soil. Or the leaves may yellow—or the plant's top growth may suddenly look far too large for the pot underneath.

Whatever the signal, the plant should come out of the pot for a check of its root ball. If the roots turn out to be thickly matted and coiling around the ball, repotting is clearly in order. For the best techniques, see below and on the opposite page.

There are a few general rules to follow. First, a plant should be repotted only when it is growing vigorously—in spring or summer. Second, a plant should not be moved into a new pot several sizes larger than the old one. The roots will take so long to stretch into the extra space that water will gather there, and the excess moisture can cause the roots to rot. The best method is to select a new pot that is only 1 to 2 inches wider measured at the rim than the old one. A pot this size should provide plenty of room for at least one season's new growth.

A last rule: always replant in a clean container. Even a new pot can benefit from a good rinse. If the chosen pot has been used before, scrub it out with a mild solution of water and bleach, to get rid of residual salts and any lingering diseases.

Three variegated dwarf scheffleras—identical plants, but different in age and size—stand in look-alike pots of staggered sizes, each appropriate to the plant it holds.

1 Before repotting your plant, moisten the soil. Then place your hand over the soil surface, supporting the stem or stems between your fingers *(right)*. Turn the pot upside down and slide the plant out. If it resists, gently rap the pot. Because repotting is best done quickly, have the new pot handy.

2 Using both hands, lightly loosen the root ball of the freed plant. This will stimulate new growth and get rid of some old soil and tired roots. It will also help shake out excess salts that can be left behind by fertilizers or by the saline "hard" water found in many localities.

3 Drop fresh potting mixture by the handful into the new container until it is about one-third full. Tamp down the mixture, but do not pack it tightly.

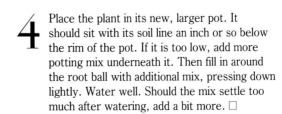

4 Place the plant in its new, larger pot. It should sit with its soil line an inch or so below the rim of the pot. If it is too low, add more potting mix underneath it. Then fill in around the root ball with additional mix, pressing down lightly. Water well. Should the mix settle too much after watering, add a bit more. □

STERILE SOIL
FOR A GOOD START

The essential ingredient in first-rate potting mixtures—the medium houseplants grow in—is not some exotic compound but rather simple soil. Partly composed of organic matter, proper soil has the nutrients that plants need for healthy growth. The best way to get some is to spade it up from the back corner of a garden; the richer brown-black it is in color, the better. Or soil can be bought in sacks from garden supply centers. Commercial soil may not be as rich as the garden variety, but it comes bagged and is easy to obtain and handle.

Both sorts, though, need some doctoring before being used. First, garden soil may contain organisms harmful to plants—and so may commercial soil unless it is labeled "sterile." The remedy is to heat the soil in an oven, as shown on the opposite page. This easy procedure eliminates harmful organisms in the soil. Its only drawback is that the soil, while heating, emits an unpleasant odor.

Second, the soil's texture will need some improving. In addition to organic matter, all soils contain sand and clay. Too much clay means a heavy, sticky soil that drains poorly. The answer here is to blend in handfuls of sand or a soil conditioner, such as perlite. Loose, sandy soil, by contrast, has little water-holding capacity. It can be made more water-retentive by working in vermiculite or peat moss.

A third concern: various types of plants prefer soils of different textures. Cacti, for example, dislike having wet roots, so they need a sandy, lighter-than-normal mix. The box at right offers recipes for soil mixes to suit three basic kinds of houseplants.

Potting soil that has been sterilized and amended with organic matter and a soil conditioner provides the ideal growing environment for a young, thriving caladium.

RECIPES FOR PLANTING MIXES

Most leafy houseplants grow best in a mixture that retains some moisture but also drains adequately. The formula for this average mix is given below. Cacti and succulents prefer a drier mixture *(center),* and ferns a moisture-retentive compound *(right).* In all, the soil is enriched with organic materials. For the requirements of specific plants, consult the dictionary on pages 96-135.

ALL-PURPOSE MIX

1 part soil

1 part peat moss

1 part perlite or coarse sand

MIX FOR CACTI AND SUCCULENTS

1 part soil

1 part peat moss

2 parts coarse sand

MIX FOR FERNS AND OTHER MOISTURE LOVERS

1 part soil

3 parts peat moss

1 part vermiculite

1 After preheating your oven to about 200° F, mound up several good handfuls of garden earth (or commercial potting soil) in a shallow baking dish. Cover the soil with a sheet of aluminum foil. Crimp the foil over the edges of the pan, making as tight a seal as you can.

2 Stick a meat thermometer in the soil and place the pan in the oven. Watch the thermometer, making sure it registers at least 150° F. To eliminate harmful soil organisms and retain helpful ones, the soil should bake at between 150° and 180° for 30 minutes. If the oven runs hot and the soil reaches 180° after 20 minutes or so, turn the oven off but leave the pan inside the oven for the remaining 10 minutes.

3 When you have taken the pan from the oven, let the soil cool—keeping the foil cover in place— for a couple of hours. Once it has cooled, the soil is ready to be mixed with other ingredients *(box, opposite)*, or it can be stored in an airtight container for use in the future. □

11

HOUSEPLANTS
AND THEIR DIVERSE HABITS

A corn plant, a Chinese evergreen, a snake plant, a dumbcane, a piggyback plant and a dracaena (clockwise from top left) share the subdued light of a shuttered windowsill. All are members of the diverse group known as green plants.

The term "houseplants" covers a wide range of growing things from delicate ferns to spiky cacti, from low-growing succulents to high-spiraling vines. Plants belonging to dozens of botanical families and many thousands of species can be and are cultivated indoors. About all they have in common is that they will flourish in the subdued light and year-round warmth of a house.

This great wealth of plant life can nevertheless be divided for convenience into six major groupings—as seen at right and on the next two pages. These divisions take liberties with the scholarly distinctions that botanists make between genera. Only three of the categories found here, the cacti, the bromeliads and the palms, are in fact made up of members of single, distinct botanical families. The other three groupings—the green plants, ferns and succulents—may combine two or more different families.

Still, these broad groupings can be highly useful. Each category is made up of plants that share many physical characteristics. Many originated in similar natural environments. This is vital information for the indoor gardener because species that resemble one another, and derive from the same habitats, will inevitably require the same kind of indoor environment—sunny or shady, warm or cool—and similar amounts of water, fertilizer and other sorts of care.

GREEN OR FOLIAGE PLANTS

All plants valued especially for their green and often large-leaved foliage, such as the Swiss cheese plant, the grassy-leaved sweet flag and the philodendron shown at left, are often lumped under the heading "green plants" by nursery owners and other horticulturists. Put another way, green plants include almost any decorative varieties that do not belong in the other five categories pictured here and on the following pages. Mostly originating in subtropical climates, these staples of indoor gardening tolerate a wide range of light and moisture conditions, and will do well in an average home without a lot of special attention.

FERNS

There are many species of ferns, but generally they divide into two sorts, the epiphytic and the terrestrial. In the wild, the epiphytes grow in the air, or rather, cling in the crevices of trees, drawing nourishment from the rotting vegetation trapped there. Terrestrials normally grow in the soil on the forest floor. Indoors, many epiphytes will grow in pots. Both types, being adapted to shadowy, woodsy environments, grow best in dappled light and humid air, and need soil that is rich in organic matter.

CACTI

Most members of the cactus family are native to desert areas and therefore grow best in hot, dry conditions. Their spines are actually leaves—with minimal surface area from which moisture can escape. The bodies of cacti are nothing more than hugely enlarged stems designed by nature to absorb and hold water from infrequent rainfalls. It follows, then, that cacti need generous but infrequent waterings (daily sprinklings only cause rot) and loose, well-drained soil. They also need warmth and are among the few houseplants that thrive in extended periods of direct sunlight.

SUCCULENTS

Hundreds of quite disparate-looking species are called succulents. Many not only have thickish, fleshy stems, but also chubby, water-storing leaves like those of the jade plant at right. Others have spiny leaves almost like those on cacti and still others look like (and, in fact, are) small trees. Most originated in arid parts of the world—thus their water-conserving structures. They require infrequent watering, warm temperatures, low humidity and well-drained soil.

BROMELIADS

These curious plants are related to the pineapple, and the leaves of many of them, like those of a pineapple's top, rise in a rosette pattern from a central base. The leaves are generally stiff and leathery; the flowers spring up from the cup in the middle of the rosette. In their native tropics, many bromeliads are tree-growing epiphytes, living on the rainwater and leafy debris the cups collect. As houseplants, many bromeliads continue to take in moisture through the cuplike formation at the base of their leaves and should be watered accordingly. And being tropical plants, they also need warm temperatures and high humidity.

PALMS

The palm family of plants includes more than 200 genera and a staggering 3,000 species. In the wild they have tall, single unbranched trunks topped by fans of usually broad, flat leaves. But grown as houseplants, they rarely reach maturity and thus remain compact, often with leaves and leafy branches all the way up their trunks, like the parlor palm at right. Coming from warm climates as they do, palms need regular watering, well-drained soil, average warmth and humidity, and bright sunlight. □

THREE WAYS
TO WATER YOUR HOUSEPLANTS

The crisp leaves and upright bearing of this 'Silver Queen' Chinese evergreen indicate a well-watered plant. Proper moisture balance is maintained by means of a wick that draws water from a bowl concealed underneath the lower pot into the soil of the upper pot.

Water is the lifeblood of all plants. It dissolves nutrients and transports them from the soil to the roots and from there to stems, branches and foliage. In addition, internal water pressure helps keep stems and leaves full and firm. A plant that lacks water begins to wilt and eventually dies. For many plants the soil should be kept constantly moist; for others—mainly cacti and succulents—it should dry out between waterings.

There are three ways to water. One is to pour water onto the soil from above until it begins to run out the drainage holes at the bottom of the pot. If you use this method, sprinkle slowly and gently with a watering can; do not flood the pot with a blast from the water tap. Another is to set the pot in a pan of water and let the moisture rise into the soil from below. When the soil surface is moist, the plant has had enough and should be removed from the pan. Never let plants sit in water longer than necessary. If the roots become waterlogged, they will eventually rot and the plant will die.

A third method of watering is by means of a wick—a length of twine made of cotton or other natural fiber. The wick draws moisture up into the soil slowly and continuously from a reservoir maintained beneath the pot. The method is especially useful if you have to be away from home for a period of time. Wicking is also an easy way of providing low-maintenance regular care for plants such as ferns and baby's tears, which do best when their soil is kept constantly moist. The method can be used with any plants except cacti and succulents.

Because you will sometimes be combining fertilizing with watering, no matter which method you use, whitish salts will accumulate on the soil surface and the pot rim from time to time and, if left too long, may burn plant tissues. Whenever you find such a buildup, place your plants under a tap and let water drain through the soil several times.

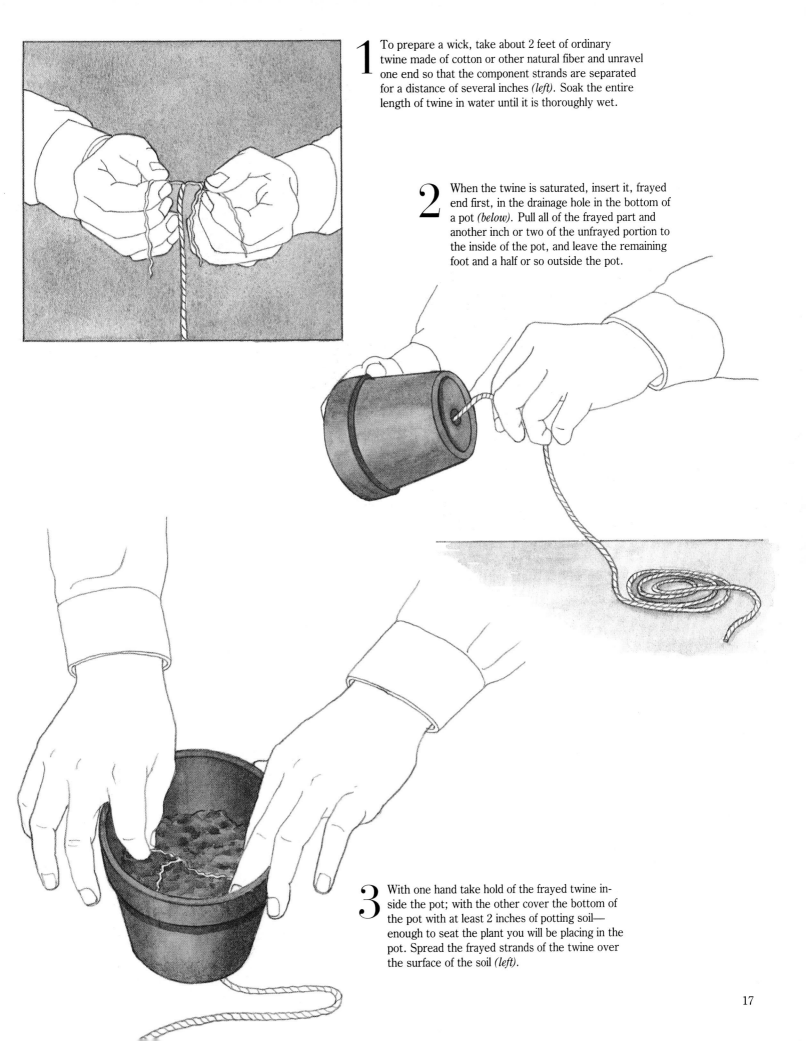

1 To prepare a wick, take about 2 feet of ordinary twine made of cotton or other natural fiber and unravel one end so that the component strands are separated for a distance of several inches *(left)*. Soak the entire length of twine in water until it is thoroughly wet.

2 When the twine is saturated, insert it, frayed end first, in the drainage hole in the bottom of a pot *(below)*. Pull all of the frayed part and another inch or two of the unfrayed portion to the inside of the pot, and leave the remaining foot and a half or so outside the pot.

3 With one hand take hold of the frayed twine inside the pot; with the other cover the bottom of the pot with at least 2 inches of potting soil—enough to seat the plant you will be placing in the pot. Spread the frayed strands of the twine over the surface of the soil *(left)*.

4 Place the plant in the pot, making sure it sits at the same level as it did in its previous pot. Add more soil and pack it down around the roots *(left)*. The soil surface should be about 1 inch below the rim of the pot. Pour water on the soil until it starts to drain from the hole in the bottom.

5 Turn a large, empty flower pot upside down and place it on a counter. Thread the unfrayed end of the twine through the drainage hole in the overturned pot *(right)* until you have taken up all the slack. The twine will form a loose coil on the counter under the big pot.

6 Fill a bowl with water to serve as a reservoir. Pull the twine from under the big pot and submerge it in the water. Set the potted plant over the overturned pot so that the twine runs unimpeded through the two drainage holes and into the water *(left)*. Then set the two pots on top of the bowl of water, making sure the twine remains submerged in the water. The wick will draw water up from the reservoir and into the potting soil. Check the soil surface periodically; refill the reservoir when necessary. □

LIQUID   POWDER   SPIKES   BEADS

ABOUT FERTILIZERS From time to time your plants will need fertilizing—not to stimulate growth, but to maintain good condition; they will need nitrogen for healthy foliage, phosphorus for strong roots and potassium for overall vigor. A 1:1:1 or 1:2:1 ratio of those ingredients is best for houseplants. Fertilizers come in several forms—liquid, water-soluble powder, timed-release spikes and beads—and the nutrients of all are distributed to plant tissues by means of water. Spikes and beads are inserted in soil that is moist; the liquids and powders should be mixed with water before being applied.

A PEBBLE TRAY
TO PROVIDE HUMIDITY

Side by side, two hybrid caladiums of contrasting colors thrive in the elevated humidity provided by vapor rising from the moistened pebble tray they share.

Most plants like moist air. They are constantly losing water to the air through their leaves, in a process called transpiration. When the surrounding air is laden with moisture, transpiration slows down and plants find it easier to maintain a healthy water balance.

Atmospheric moisture is measured in terms of relative humidity. The ability of air to hold water vapor varies with temperature; the warmer the air, the more vapor it can hold. To determine the level of humidity you need a hygrometer—an instrument that measures the percentage of moisture in the air. A reading of 100 percent would mean complete saturation. You can buy this useful and inexpensive instrument at garden centers.

Most houseplants grow best when the relative humidity is about 50 percent—considerably higher than the 10 to 20 percent relative humidity of most homes, especially during winter. Fortunately, there are ways to keep the air around your plants moist.

A portable electric humidifier can raise the relative humidity in its immediate vicinity to between 30 and 60 percent. Grouping plants closely together on a table or shelf creates a moister microclimate in which each plant benefits from its neighbors' water loss.

Plants suffering from dry air may start to wither prematurely; spraying a fine mist in the air around the plants from a plastic or metal mister brings temporary relief. With all plants but bromeliads *(page 74)*, avoid drenching the leaves, as this can cause spotting and increase susceptibility to disease. Plants with fuzzy leaves should never be misted at all.

The easiest and most reliable way to give your plants the humidity they need is to place them in a pebble tray, which provides moisture through evaporation.

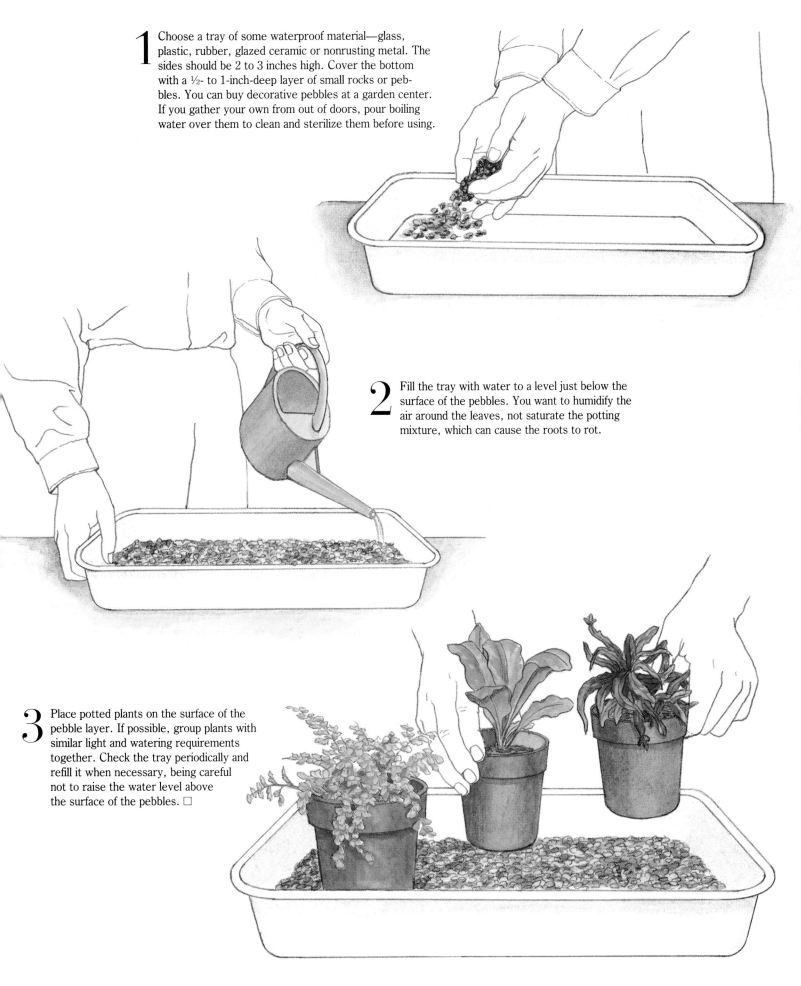

1 Choose a tray of some waterproof material—glass, plastic, rubber, glazed ceramic or nonrusting metal. The sides should be 2 to 3 inches high. Cover the bottom with a ½- to 1-inch-deep layer of small rocks or pebbles. You can buy decorative pebbles at a garden center. If you gather your own from out of doors, pour boiling water over them to clean and sterilize them before using.

2 Fill the tray with water to a level just below the surface of the pebbles. You want to humidify the air around the leaves, not saturate the potting mixture, which can cause the roots to rot.

3 Place potted plants on the surface of the pebble layer. If possible, group plants with similar light and watering requirements together. Check the tray periodically and refill it when necessary, being careful not to raise the water level above the surface of the pebbles. □

PLACING PLANTS IN THE RIGHT LIGHT

An arrowhead vine grows green and bushy in its west-facing "summer residence." Sheer curtains on either side diffuse the afternoon sunlight that floods the bay window.

Three factors—light, water and nutrients—are vital for thriving plants. Of the three, the most difficult to supply in just the right amount is light. A plant that is starved for light eventually grows weak and spindly; its leaves turn pale and fall off. At the other extreme, too much light causes leaves to wilt and fade, or to be stunted in growth.

Houseplants can tolerate less-than-ideal growing conditions; that is why they were chosen as houseplants in the first place. Yet most prefer lighting that closely approximates their native habitats—dim forest floors, tree-dotted savannas, sun-scorched deserts.

Where you place a plant in your house determines how much light it will receive at a specific time of the year. Rooms that bask in a full day's sun in summer may see only a few hours of winter sunlight. Many houseplants adjust to diminished light by slowing their growth; some even require an annual period of rest. Others benefit greatly if they are moved around the house to "follow the sun."

For a guide to the seasonal migration of sunlight, see the opposite page. Each circle is divided into quadrants to represent the points of the compass. The small rectangle in the center of each represents a house. Flowerpots in the quadrants indicate which seasonal exposure will provide one of three light levels. For the preferences of specific plants, consult the Dictionary of Houseplants *(pages 96-135).*

In locations with little or no natural light, you can raise plants under artificial light, preferably fluorescent bulbs that deliver a kind of imitation sunlight. Place the bulbs 18 to 24 inches above the plants; leave them on 12 to 16 hours a day.

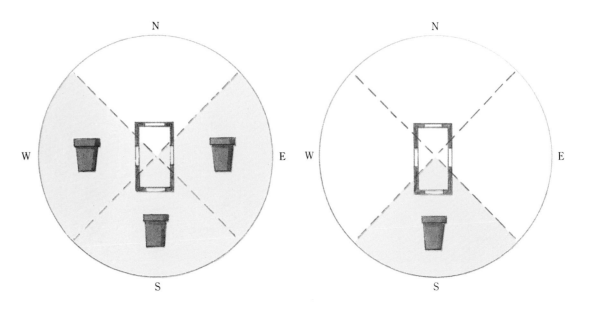

DIRECT LIGHT

The sun strikes foliage for at least four hours a day. Direct light is found in summer in unobstructed, uncurtained east-, west- and south-facing windows *(right)*, but only in south-facing windows in winter *(far right)*. It is suited to plants of desert origin.

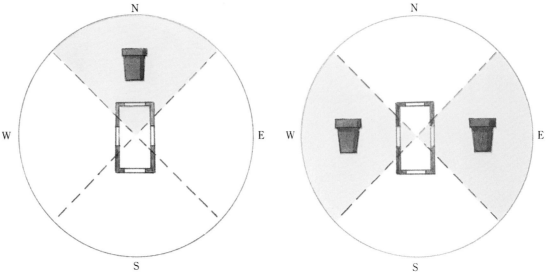

BRIGHT LIGHT

The sun strikes foliage for less than four hours, but at least one hour a day. Bright light is found in unobstructed, uncurtained north-facing windows in summer *(right)*; in east- and west-facing windows in winter *(far right)*. Most house-plants do well in this type of light.

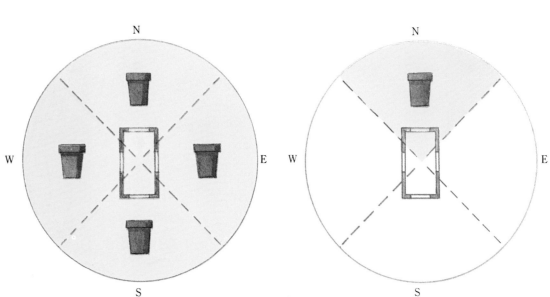

LIMITED LIGHT

The sun rarely strikes foliage directly. Limited light is found in any exposure in summer *(right)* if you place plants 5 feet from un-obstructed windows or hang sheer curtains; in winter *(far right)* it is found on north-facing window-sills. It is suited to plants that grow naturally in jungles and on forest floors. □

PINCHING AND PRUNING
FOR HANDSOME AND HEALTHY GROWTH

With its lush green leaves and small white flower buds, a Tahitian bridal veil covers a side table. The plant's dense foliage and compact, mounded shape are the result of regular pinching.

Many houseplants as they mature stretch upward too swiftly toward the light—and become overly tall and scraggly with few lower branches and sparse foliage. Or sometimes branches shoot out too far, throwing the plants out of balance and spoiling their shape.

Happily there are two parallel remedies for these awkward developments. The simpler of the two is pinching, which means using the fingers to remove the fresh new tips that grow on the ends of stems and branches. Such minor surgery spurs the growth of otherwise dormant buds farther down the stalks. The result: new branches, thicker foliage and generally more compact, bushy, handsome plants. Timely pinching may produce such full, thick and shapely results that pruning will not be necessary.

But sometimes pruning is necessary; it is, in fact, just a more radical version of pinching. It involves using garden shears or clippers to snip stems and branches too thick or too woody for finger and thumb. The main idea is to reshape a plant that has grown irregularly and make it more symmetrical. But the effect can also be the same as pinching, stirring dormant buds into life and promoting fresh, healthy growth. Shears and clippers, however, can spread plant diseases, so sterilize them between operations by dipping them in a solution of one part bleach and nine parts water.

The best time of year for either process is early spring, when plants have plenty of energy to produce new growth swiftly.

Most houseplants respond well to pinching and pruning, but some cannot stand either. Most of the latter are ones that have a single growing stem—palms, corn plants and Norfolk Island pines, for example.

JUDICIOUS SNIPPING FOR WAYWARD BRANCHES

Houseplants that are small trees, such as the jade shown here, can especially benefit from periodic pruning. If a branch sticks out awkwardly, snip it back. Also cut off any weak or unhealthy branches in the center of the plant, to open it up to light and air. Cut ½ inch or less above a node—where a leaf or a pair of leaves emerge from the stem.

PINCHING FOR FULLER FOLIAGE

Fingers and thumbnail are the best tools for pinching back the tender new stem tips produced by such plants as the wandering Jew shown here. After a first round of pinching has encouraged the growth of several fresh stems or branches, you can pinch off their tips to promote still fuller, denser growth. ☐

KEEPING PLANT GROWTH UNDER CONTROL

A weeping fig tree stands in perfect proportion to its location in a sunlit corner of a dining room. The tree has been kept at this size by periodic trimming of the roots and repotting in the same container.

Suppose one of the larger woody houseplants—a weeping fig, say, or a schefflera—has grown to the perfect height for its place in a room. It looks ideal standing in its sunny corner—and yet new top growth shows signs of wanting to reach the ceiling; at the same time some yellowing leaves indicate that the roots are cramped in their pot and need more space.

What *not* to do in this case is repot the plant in a larger container. A larger container would afford the roots more room and restore the plant's vigor—but it would also encourage the plant to outgrow the space where it looks so comfortably at home.

The answer is to employ the method shown at right of repotting the plant in the same container. The object is to maintain the plant's health while keeping its growth under control.

Moving a plant only to put it back where it was has its strenuous element, which begins with getting a large, mature plant out of its pot—a task made easier if a second person helps. Then the crowded roots will need some rather drastic knife work if, put back in the same container, they are to have enough room to grow. Finally, some judicious pruning of the foliage will be required to bring the plant back into balance with its reduced root system. But if the plant grows from a single stem, as palms do, the foliage should not be pruned.

The equipment needed is simple: a rather large, sharp knife for the roots and some bleach-and-water solution in which to sterilize the blade; a pair of small pruning shears; and some old newspapers to spread over the working area, since the process causes considerable fallout from old roots and potting soil.

The best times of year for this sort of repotting are late fall and winter, when the plant is dormant and the shock suffered by a root ball during moving and handling is less than in spring and summer, when it is growing.

1 Before removing the plant from its pot, water it; a moist root ball will slip out more easily than a dry one. Then, if the plant is large, tip it on its side and ease the root ball onto a sheet of newspaper. Should the roots prove stubborn and cling to the pot, you can loosen them by tapping the pot gently with a rubber mallet.

2 Once the plant is out of its pot, use a knife to shave away about an inch of old soil and roots all the way around the side of the root ball. At the same time you can use your fingers to unwind long, clinging roots and generally rough up the sides of the ball, which helps promote new root growth.

3 Gently lower the newly shaved root ball back into the pot, filling the extra space around it with fresh potting soil. Firm the soil with your hands, adding more if necessary. The plant should sit at the same level as it did before.

4 Using sterilized clippers, prune some foliage to make up for the root loss. For indoor trees of moderate size (as shown), trim about 10 branches back a few inches. Always make the cut just above a node *(pages 24-25)*. □

2
REJUVENATING AND REPLICATING

Almost every schoolchild knows that plants can be grown from seed. Witness the brave little soil-filled milk cartons sporting zinnia seedlings that line schoolroom windows. Less well known is the fact that many plants are able to reproduce themselves from the most unlikely bits and pieces of their anatomy—from leafstalks and leaf veins; from the tips of plant stems; from sections called rhizomes, which look like roots but are actually stems. The offspring of such plant parts always duplicate the parent plant exactly, a particularly useful trait when the plant is cherished for its color or form, as houseplants often are. Simultaneously, such methods of plant propagation can improve the health of pot-grown plants that have become spindly with age or whose roots overcrowd their containers.

An array of these reproductive techniques is explored on the following pages, beginning with the familiar process of growing plants from seed, and ending with instructions for producing a pineapple plant from the discarded crown of a freshly cut pineapple. In between are explanations for how to grow plants from stem cuttings, for example, and from two kinds of leaf cuttings: in one method, roots grow from the base of a leafstalk, and in the other, roots grow from the veins of a leaf. There are instructions for a technique called layering, acquiring new plants from the anchoring roots that are found along the stems of such climbing plants as philodendron and ivy. Another technique, called air layering, encourages roots to form from nicks cut into, but not through, such thick-stemmed plants as rubber trees and dumbcane.

Happily, none of this horticultural tinkering requires any special equipment. For most of it, all that is needed is a sterile propagating medium for the young plants, clean pots and clean tools, and occasionally a rooting compound to speed the action. Also helpful is a steady warmth—which can often be provided by improvising a miniature greenhouse out of a plastic bag.

STARTING
HOUSEPLANTS FROM SEEDS

Two rows of eight-week-old mimosa seedlings stand in a shaft of sunlight coming from a distant window. Young seedlings can take up to four hours of morning sunlight each day.

One of the most enjoyable and inexpensive ways to fill your house with plants is to start them from seed. The seeds of most common houseplants are readily available from seed catalogs, and the more exotic varieties can be ordered through specialized plant societies.

Among the easiest houseplants to grow from seed are bromeliads, coleus and philodendrons; their seeds absorb water rapidly, which encourages germination. The seeds should be planted in a fresh, sterile medium. Vermiculite is a good choice, since it holds water well, provides good aeration and is light enough for young roots and shoots to penetrate.

Details of planting vary. As a rule of thumb, large seeds need to embedded about ½ inch deep in the medium. Others, generally very tiny ones, like those of coleus, will germinate only if they are exposed to light. Check the seed packet for information on your specific plants. If your seeds need to be exposed, don't bury them in the medium; just make a slight indentation in the surface and drop the seeds in.

Once the seeds are planted, they must be kept moist at all times; if they dry out even briefly, they will not sprout. For this reason, plastic trays and pots are best for starting seeds. Clay containers are porous; they allow water to evaporate through the sides, which may leave the propagating medium too dry.

For most plants, an even temperature between 70° and 75° F is ideal for germination. To help maintain a warm temperature, place the trays of planted seeds on top of your refrigerator until germination begins.

Once the seeds have sprouted, they will need enough light to keep them from becoming weak and spindly. Prolonged exposure to direct sun can damage the tender new leaf tissue; bright sunlight is best. (For differences between various levels of light, see page 22.) If your light indoors is limited, it can be supplemented with artificial light. Fluorescent lamps located 6 to 8 inches above the seedlings will supply adequate light.

1 Select a plastic tray with drainage holes in the bottom. Fill the tray with at least 2 inches of vermiculite. Place the tray in a larger container of water *(right);* the vermiculite will absorb water through the drainage holes. When the surface of the vermiculite darkens (indicating it is saturated), remove the plastic tray from the larger container. Allow excess water to drain away.

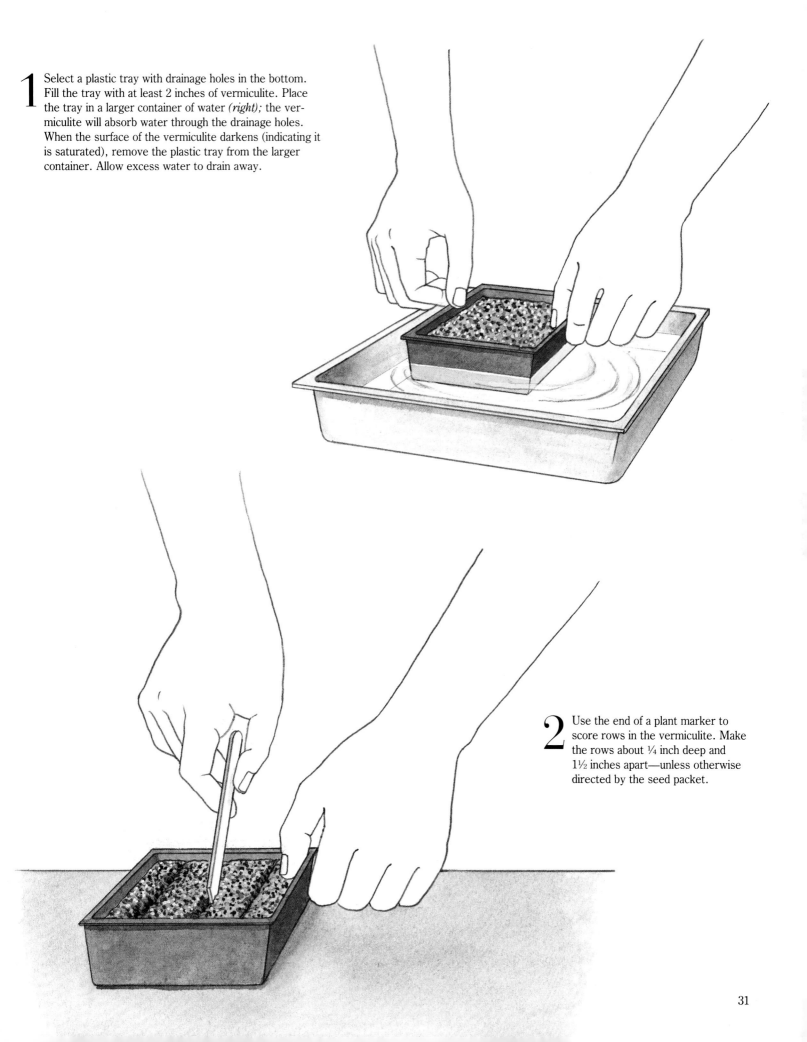

2 Use the end of a plant marker to score rows in the vermiculite. Make the rows about ¼ inch deep and 1½ inches apart—unless otherwise directed by the seed packet.

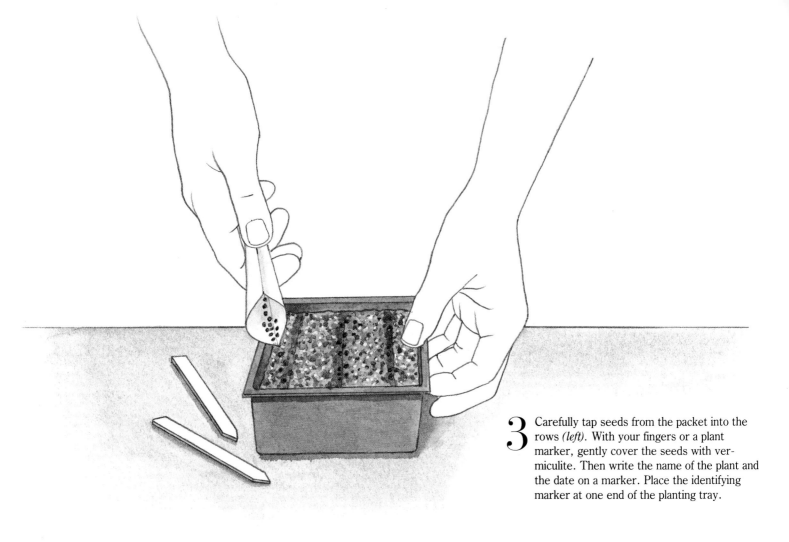

3 Carefully tap seeds from the packet into the rows *(left)*. With your fingers or a plant marker, gently cover the seeds with vermiculite. Then write the name of the plant and the date on a marker. Place the identifying marker at one end of the planting tray.

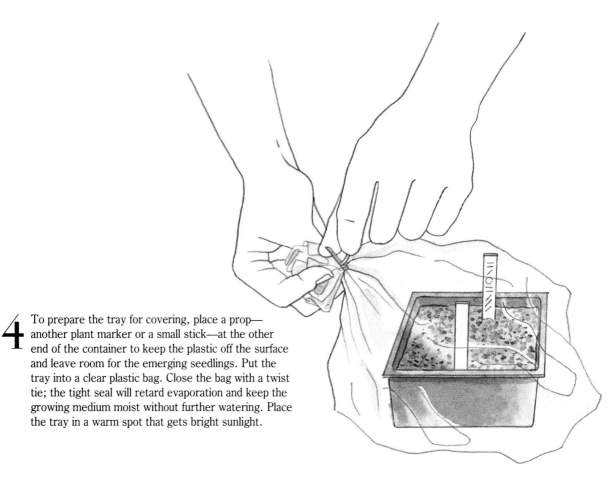

4 To prepare the tray for covering, place a prop—another plant marker or a small stick—at the other end of the container to keep the plastic off the surface and leave room for the emerging seedlings. Put the tray into a clear plastic bag. Close the bag with a twist tie; the tight seal will retard evaporation and keep the growing medium moist without further watering. Place the tray in a warm spot that gets bright sunlight.

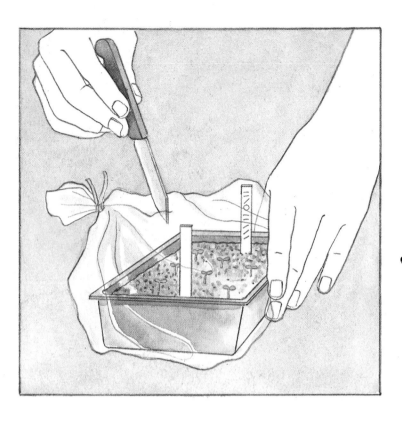

5 When the seeds begin to sprout, poke several small holes in the plastic bag *(left)*. Exposing the seedlings to some outside air will begin their gradual process of adaptation to a less sheltered environment. As the seedlings get bigger, poke additional holes in the plastic.

6 To prevent overcrowding, thin the rows by plucking out excess plants; there should be at least ½ inch between seedlings. After thinning, return the tray to the plastic bag, reseal it and continue adding holes. When the seedlings produce their second set of leaves— usually after six to eight weeks—remove the tray from the plastic. Transplant the seedlings to individual pots *(page 34)*. □

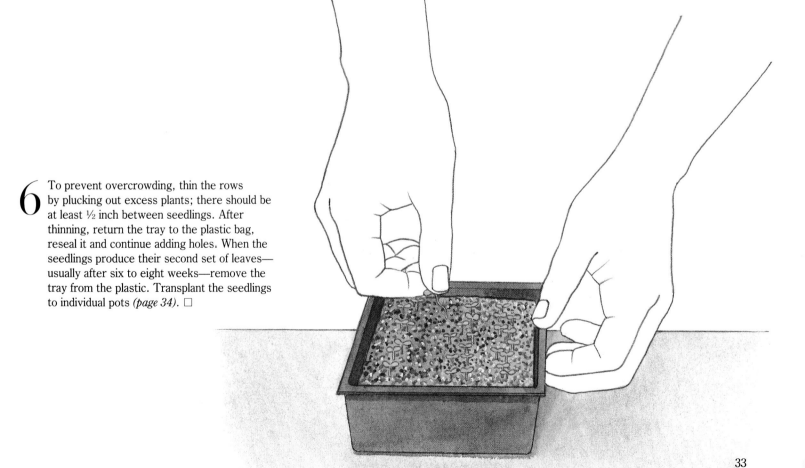

TRANSPLANTING SEEDLINGS AND CUTTINGS

Several-month-old pink-and-green polka-dot plants—weaned from a sterile rooting mix in which they were begun as seeds, and transplanted into individual pots—grow vigorously. Seedlings can be moved to 2-inch pots as soon as they develop a second pair of leaves, a sign that strong roots have developed.

Seedlings and cuttings get a good start in life when raised in soilless rooting mixes. These mixes are sterile, which reduces the risk of disease, and their loose texture allows easy penetration by tender new roots. As soon as the roots are sturdy enough, however, the plants should be moved to soil that contains all the nutrients needed for continued healthy growth.

Look for signs that tell you when to transplant. A seedling is ready when a second pair of leaves appears on the stem. A cutting is ready when new growth appears on top or when the plant offers resistance to a gentle tug.

Once these signs of root development appear, don't wait too long to move plants; the larger the roots get, the greater the danger of injuring them in the moving process.

Cuttings tend to be less fragile than seedlings, but both should be handled with care and the transplanting should be prepared for, several hours in advance. First, water seedlings and cuttings thoroughly to allow them to absorb all the moisture they can hold; dry roots are especially brittle. Then, before digging up seedlings and cuttings, be sure you have new pots ready to receive them; the less time they are exposed to the air the better, because roots begin to dry out the moment they are uncovered. Fill the pots with a premoistened soil mix recommended for the plants you intend to move.

The new pots should be 2 to 3 inches in diameter, depending on the size of the transplants. Avoid pots that are too large. Water tends to collect in the excess soil that young roots do not penetrate, and wet soil can cause a plant to rot.

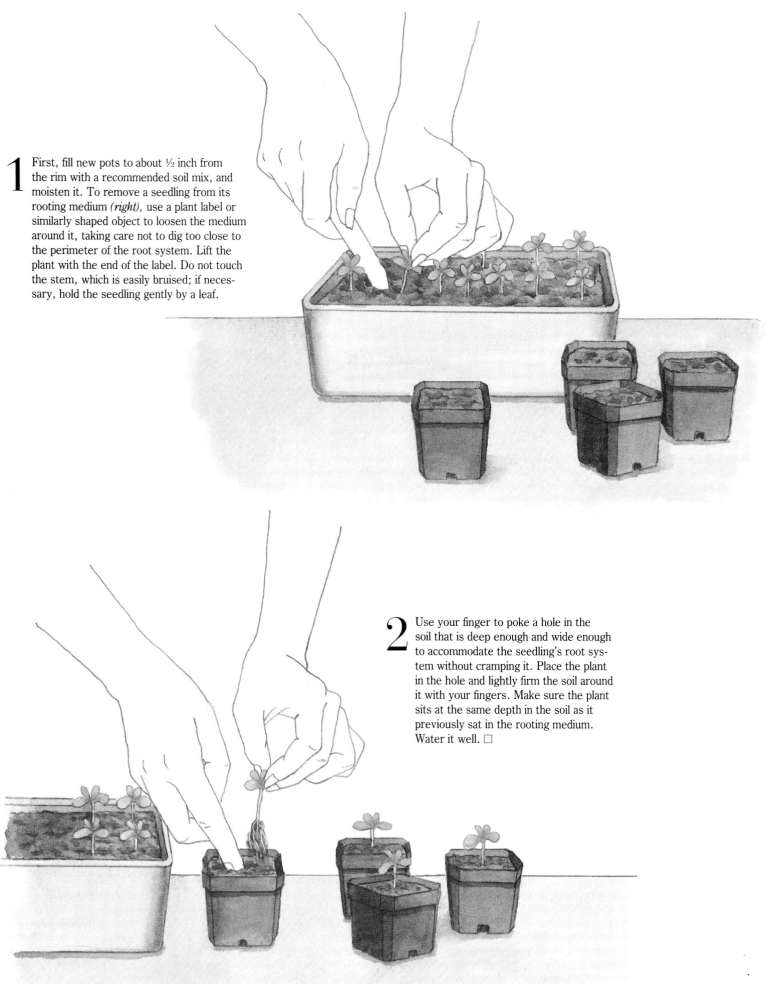

1 First, fill new pots to about ½ inch from the rim with a recommended soil mix, and moisten it. To remove a seedling from its rooting medium *(right),* use a plant label or similarly shaped object to loosen the medium around it, taking care not to dig too close to the perimeter of the root system. Lift the plant with the end of the label. Do not touch the stem, which is easily bruised; if necessary, hold the seedling gently by a leaf.

2 Use your finger to poke a hole in the soil that is deep enough and wide enough to accommodate the seedling's root system without cramping it. Place the plant in the hole and lightly firm the soil around it with your fingers. Make sure the plant sits at the same depth in the soil as it previously sat in the rooting medium. Water it well. □

GROWING HOUSEPLANTS FROM STEM CUTTINGS

One of the easiest ways to increase your indoor plant collection is by taking stem cuttings and planting them in a light propagating medium in which they can take root and grow into new plants. Virtually any multistemmed plant can be propagated by this method, and the new plant will be identical to the parent plant in all characteristics —color, size and growth habits.

Cuttings are usually taken from the tip of a stem. Additional pieces cut from the middle of the stem will grow if you plant them with the original "up" end sticking up. The best time to take a stem cutting is in spring or early summer when the plant is entering its active growing period.

Look for healthy, pliable stems with clearly visible nodes—slight bumps that mark the tissue from which leaves sprout. Avoid shoots of soft new growth (the tissue is not strong enough to start producing roots) and avoid old limbs that feel dry and brittle (they may be past being able to grow roots). Cut cleanly with a sharp knife; tissue that has been torn or crushed is unlikely to root.

The propagating medium should be soilless; soil offers too much resistance to tender young roots just trying to get established. Vermiculite is ideal.

Almost any container will do, but one that will keep necessary moisture high and maintenance low is a pot-within-a-pot unit that you can put together yourself. It consists of two clay pots of different sizes—a large pot that holds a ring of rooting medium and a smaller pot that fits inside the larger pot and holds a reservoir of water, which passes through the porous sides of the pot into the rooting medium.

This attractive potpourri of foliage colors was created by combining fast-growing stem cuttings from three different coleus hybrids.

1 Fill a large clay pot about halfway to the top with dry vermiculite or with vermiculite combined with peat moss, a medium that is light enough for tender young roots to push through.

2 Plug the drainage hole in the bottom of the small pot with a fresh cork *(right)*. Be sure the cork is of a size that will make a tight seal; if necessary, start with one that is too large and pare it down with a sharp knife or a single-edged razor blade.

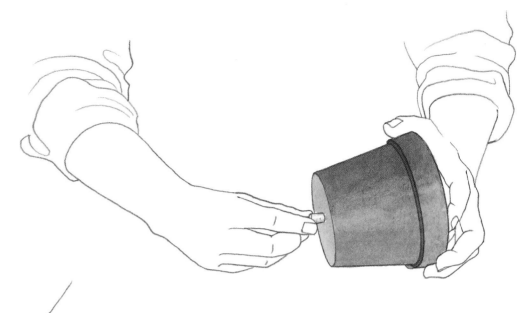

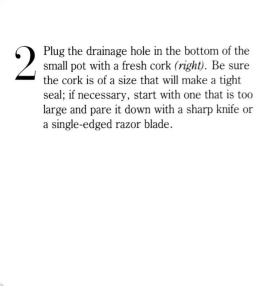

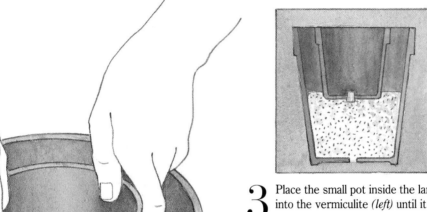

3 Place the small pot inside the large one. Push it down into the vermiculite *(left)* until it is centered and the top rims of the two pots are level with each other *(inset, above)*. Add more vermiculite to bring the medium to within about 1 inch of the rims of the pots.

4 Set the combined pots in a pan of warm water to allow the vermiculite to absorb moisture from below. Fill the inner pot with water *(right)*. When the surface of the vermiculite is fully wet, remove the entire unit from the pan and let any excess water drain out.

5 With the double-pot unit ready for use, select a healthy, pliable stem to make cuttings from the plant you wish to propagate. Each cutting should be about 4 inches long. With a sharp knife, cut below a leaf node on an angle *(right)* so that you expose as much area as possible for root formation.

6 Remove any leaves from the bottom inch or two of a cutting *(above)*. Leaves buried in the rooting medium will only rot, but the nodes left when the leaves are removed should produce viable roots.

7 For each cutting, poke a hole in the vermiculite with a pencil, a finger or a knife point. Carefully insert the cuttings in the vermiculite to a depth of 1 to 1½ inches *(right)*, and secure them in place by tamping down gently with your fingers.

8 To maintain a humid environment for the cuttings, enclose the entire unit in a large plastic bag *(above)*. Insert three or four short sticks around the rim of the pot to keep the plastic from touching the cuttings. Place the unit in a location that is bright but out of direct sunlight. Roots may form from three weeks to two months later, depending on the plant; to see if they have, check periodically by gently tugging at the base of the stems. Once the roots are strong enough to resist your pull, transplant the cuttings to individual containers filled with planting mix *(page 34)*. □

A HORMONE BOOST FOR SLOW-ROOTING STEMS

Some plants, like weeping fig, ming aralia and coffee plant, have naturally woody stems. Since these are slow to take root, you can speed up the process by applying rooting hormone powder to the cut end. Shake a very small amount from the container onto a small sheet of paper. Roll the cut end of the stem in powder and carefully tap off any excess before planting. To avoid spreading disease, do not dip cuttings into the original rooting hormone container, and throw away any excess remaining on the paper.

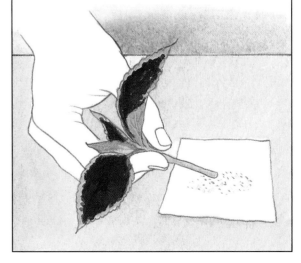

PROPAGATING FROM LEAVES AND STALKS

A crowd of green leaves interspersed with tall cream flower spikes mark a healthy, mature pixie peperomia. The leaves and leafstalks of this lush plant easily lend themselves to the leaf-and-petiole method of propagation.

P robably the easiest and most reliable way to propagate copies of a favorite houseplant is simply to cut off one or two mature leaves, usually with their stalks, or petioles (see the box at right), and stick them in a pot of propagating medium such as vermiculite. In four to six weeks, if all goes well, two or three fresh, strong and compact plantlets complete with roots will cluster about the leaves, ready for transplanting.

Not all houseplants have this capacity for producing progeny by the leaf-and-petiole method. It works well, though, with several sorts of begonias and with peperomias, seen at bottom opposite and on the following two pages.

The best sort of leaf to cut is one that has fully expanded only recently. Such a leaf, neither too young nor too old, is packed with the cells that generate new growth. The leaf should also, of course, be undamaged and not show any signs of pests or disease. Blemished leaves, like young and old ones, run the danger of rotting before producing any offspring.

You can plant leaf cuttings singly in small pots, or group several in a larger pot or in a small tray. Before you set it in pot or tray, you may dust the cut end of the stalk with rooting hormone powder. Although it is not vital, the hormone can speed the growing process.

Growing speed can also be affected by the seasons. Leaf-and-petiole cuttings can be made year round, as long as there is a fresh, fully developed leaf available. But the dimmer daylight of fall and winter will make growth slower.

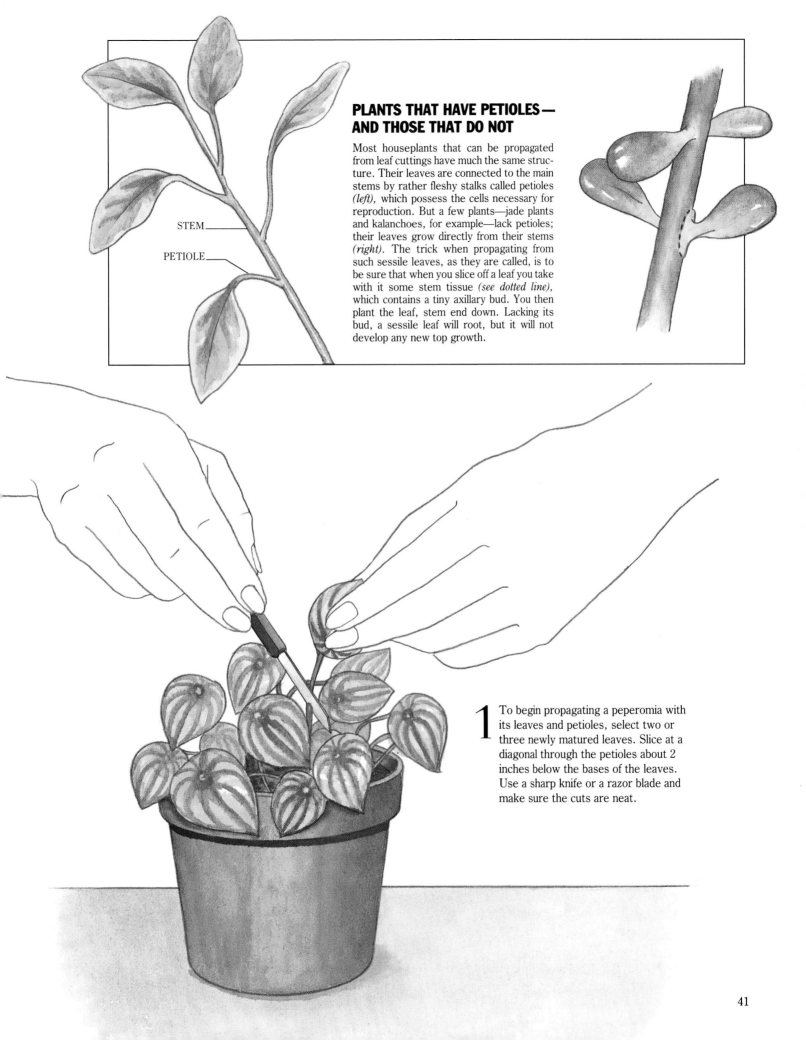

PLANTS THAT HAVE PETIOLES— AND THOSE THAT DO NOT

Most houseplants that can be propagated from leaf cuttings have much the same structure. Their leaves are connected to the main stems by rather fleshy stalks called petioles *(left)*, which possess the cells necessary for reproduction. But a few plants—jade plants and kalanchoes, for example—lack petioles; their leaves grow directly from their stems *(right)*. The trick when propagating from such sessile leaves, as they are called, is to be sure that when you slice off a leaf you take with it some stem tissue *(see dotted line)*, which contains a tiny axillary bud. You then plant the leaf, stem end down. Lacking its bud, a sessile leaf will root, but it will not develop any new top growth.

STEM

PETIOLE

1 To begin propagating a peperomia with its leaves and petioles, select two or three newly matured leaves. Slice at a diagonal through the petioles about 2 inches below the bases of the leaves. Use a sharp knife or a razor blade and make sure the cuts are neat.

41

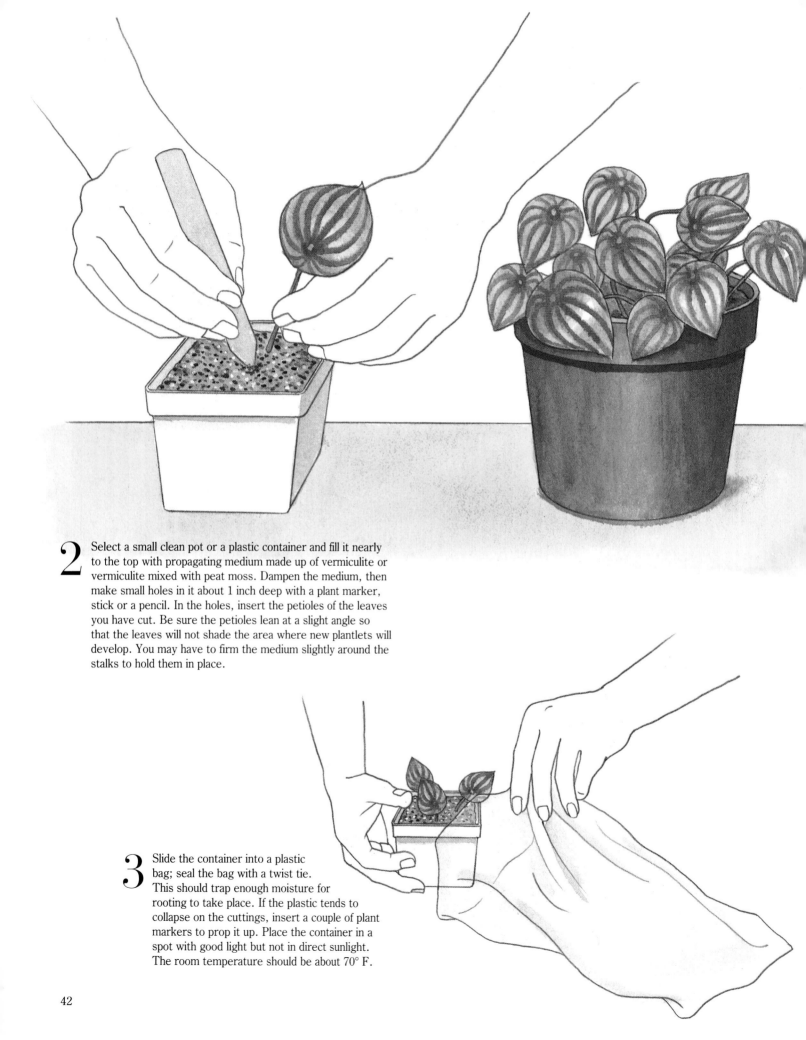

2 Select a small clean pot or a plastic container and fill it nearly
to the top with propagating medium made up of vermiculite or
vermiculite mixed with peat moss. Dampen the medium, then
make small holes in it about 1 inch deep with a plant marker,
stick or a pencil. In the holes, insert the petioles of the leaves
you have cut. Be sure the petioles lean at a slight angle so
that the leaves will not shade the area where new plantlets will
develop. You may have to firm the medium slightly around the
stalks to hold them in place.

3 Slide the container into a plastic
bag; seal the bag with a twist tie.
This should trap enough moisture for
rooting to take place. If the plastic tends to
collapse on the cuttings, insert a couple of plant
markers to prop it up. Place the container in a
spot with good light but not in direct sunlight.
The room temperature should be about 70° F.

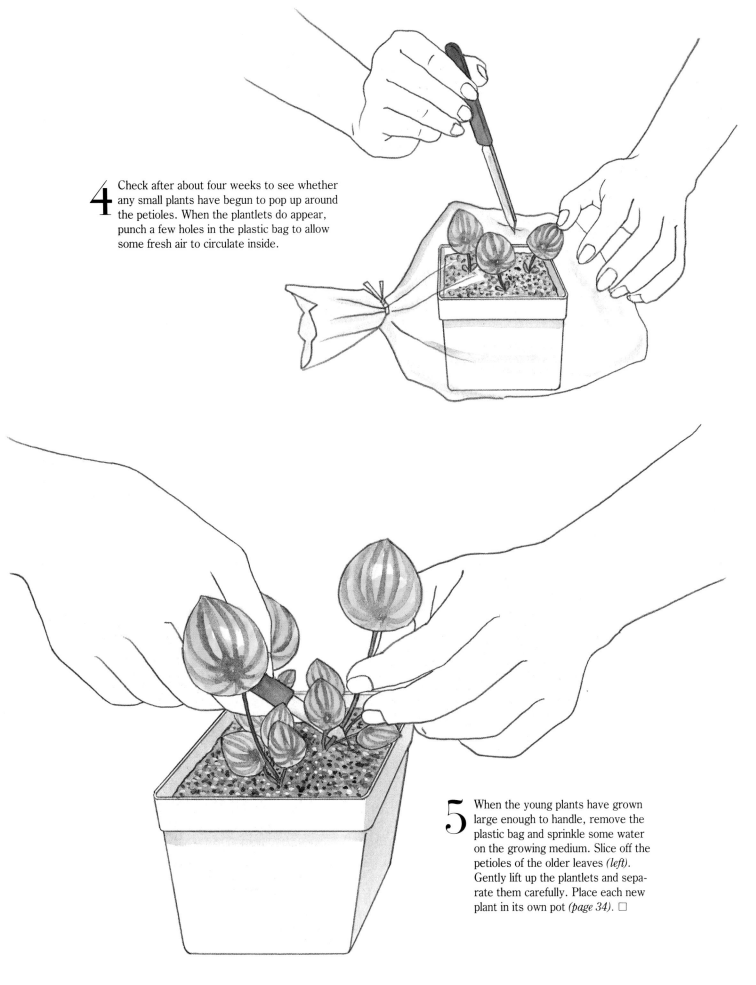

4 Check after about four weeks to see whether any small plants have begun to pop up around the petioles. When the plantlets do appear, punch a few holes in the plastic bag to allow some fresh air to circulate inside.

5 When the young plants have grown large enough to handle, remove the plastic bag and sprinkle some water on the growing medium. Slice off the petioles of the older leaves *(left)*. Gently lift up the plantlets and separate them carefully. Place each new plant in its own pot *(page 34)*. □

NEW BEGONIAS
FROM A SINGLE LEAF

Rex begonias, perhaps the most striking of all foliage houseplants with their large leaves of exotic pink, purple, silvery green, bronze and maroon, are also among the easiest to propagate, and in large numbers. They possess the astonishing ability to reproduce from the veins of their own leaves. Because begonia leaves are sizable, only one need be used for each planting. From this single leaf will spring half a dozen fresh plantlets.

Propagating rex begonias by the leaf-vein method can be done at any time of year, as long as the indoor temperature is kept around 70° F. The standard method for starting the plantlets is shown at right and on the following pages. An alternative technique is described on page 47.

As for equipment, the principal item required is a shallow pot wide enough at the top for an entire leaf to lie flat—say 6 inches across. This container should be filled with a light growing medium such as moist vermiculite or a mixture of half sand and half peat moss. Also needed is a small, sharp knife or a single-edged razor blade, and some alcohol or a mild solution of bleach to sterilize the cutting surface. Other necessities are a plastic bag large enough to fit over the pot, a few hairpins or opened paper clips to secure the leaf, and a clean surface on which to do some delicate slicing.

The only other requirement is patience; the plantlets may grow from the cuts in the veins in a month, but they may take as many as two or three months. The only real problem is finding enough window space to accommodate the flock of mature begonias the plantlets will eventually produce.

Muted reds, dusty greens and shades of silvery white adorn the crisp, intricately scalloped leaves of a rex begonia that was grown from a leaf taken from a parent plant.

1 Cut a large healthy leaf, together with its stalk, from a vigorous begonia with a sterilized knife or a razor blade. The leaf should be well grown and mature but not old. Neither elderly leaves nor very young ones propagate satisfactorily.

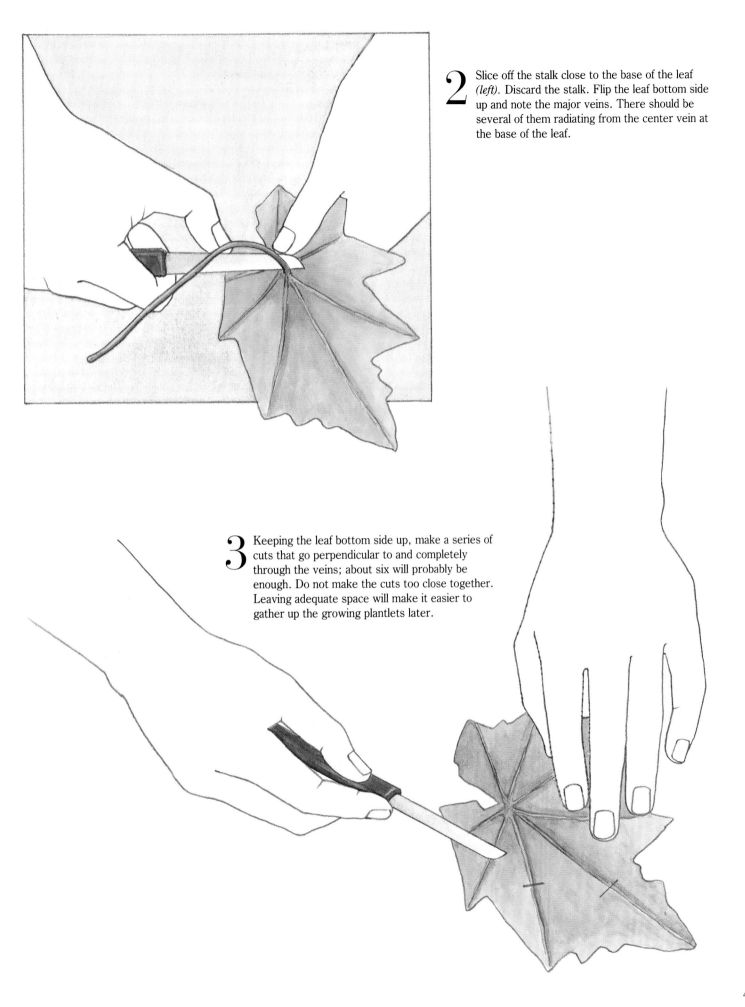

2 Slice off the stalk close to the base of the leaf *(left)*. Discard the stalk. Flip the leaf bottom side up and note the major veins. There should be several of them radiating from the center vein at the base of the leaf.

3 Keeping the leaf bottom side up, make a series of cuts that go perpendicular to and completely through the veins; about six will probably be enough. Do not make the cuts too close together. Leaving adequate space will make it easier to gather up the growing plantlets later.

4 Place the leaf face up on top of the planting medium. The cuts on the underside must be in contact with the medium in order to root. To make sure, anchor the leaf with small hairpins, opened paper clips or any other convenient fasteners.

5 Slip the pot into a plastic bag and close it tightly to form a miniature greenhouse. Place it in a bright area near a window but not in direct sunlight, which might cook the leaf and its developing progeny. When you see signs that plantlets have begun to grow, puncture the plastic to let in some fresh air.

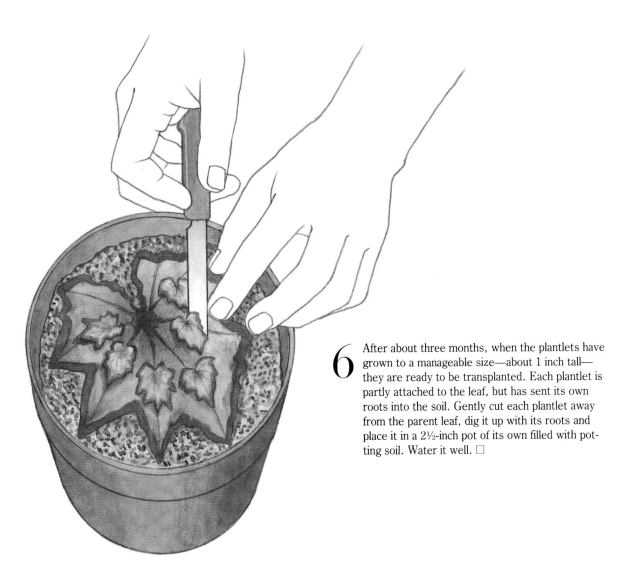

6 After about three months, when the plantlets have grown to a manageable size—about 1 inch tall—they are ready to be transplanted. Each plantlet is partly attached to the leaf, but has sent its own roots into the soil. Gently cut each plantlet away from the parent leaf, dig it up with its roots and place it in a 2½-inch pot of its own filled with potting soil. Water it well. □

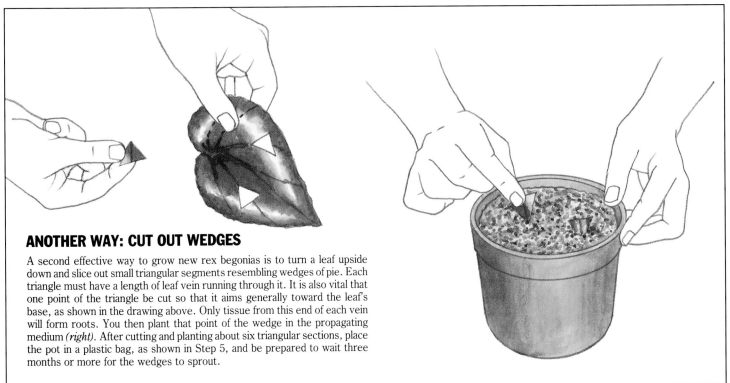

ANOTHER WAY: CUT OUT WEDGES

A second effective way to grow new rex begonias is to turn a leaf upside down and slice out small triangular segments resembling wedges of pie. Each triangle must have a length of leaf vein running through it. It is also vital that one point of the triangle be cut so that it aims generally toward the leaf's base, as shown in the drawing above. Only tissue from this end of each vein will form roots. You then plant that point of the wedge in the propagating medium *(right)*. After cutting and planting about six triangular sections, place the pot in a plastic bag, as shown in Step 5, and be prepared to wait three months or more for the wedges to sprout.

ROOTING VINES
ALONG THE SOIL LINE

A standard method of propagation is an ancient one known as layering. The technique, pictured on these pages, is quite simple: a section of stem is placed in a pot of propagating medium until it roots and starts the formation of a new little plant. Layering works with plants that have long trailing stems, among them several popular ivies, including devil's ivy, grape ivy, Swedish ivy and English ivy with its relatives of the *Hedera* genus. It is also effective with creeping fig, wandering Jew, pellionia and philodendron.

All the vines and vinelike plants listed above produce rootlets at the leaf nodes along their stems, many of them even when the stems are suspended in air. These rootlets are what enable ivy and other climbers to cling to trees and walls. Put in contact with some vermiculite mixed with peat moss, they just as readily grow downward—and produce offspring. The only supplies needed, aside from a small clean pot full of propagating mixture, are a few U-shaped hairpins or staplelike pole pins, sold at garden centers, which are used to fasten down the stem while the roots develop.

Layering can be done at any time of year, but the best seasons are spring and summer, when plants are actively growing. The process does not take long. In only three or four weeks new roots will have formed and the umbilical cord to the parent can be cut.

The long, vining stems of a lush pothos plant tumble out of a pot to drape over a wicker table. From one such stem it is easy to propagate a new pothos plant.

1 Place a small pot of vermiculite-based propagating medium near the plant—in this case a philodendron —that you wish to reproduce by layering. Bring a section of a healthy stem over to the pot and lay it on top of the medium, being sure the stem includes one or more leaf nodes.

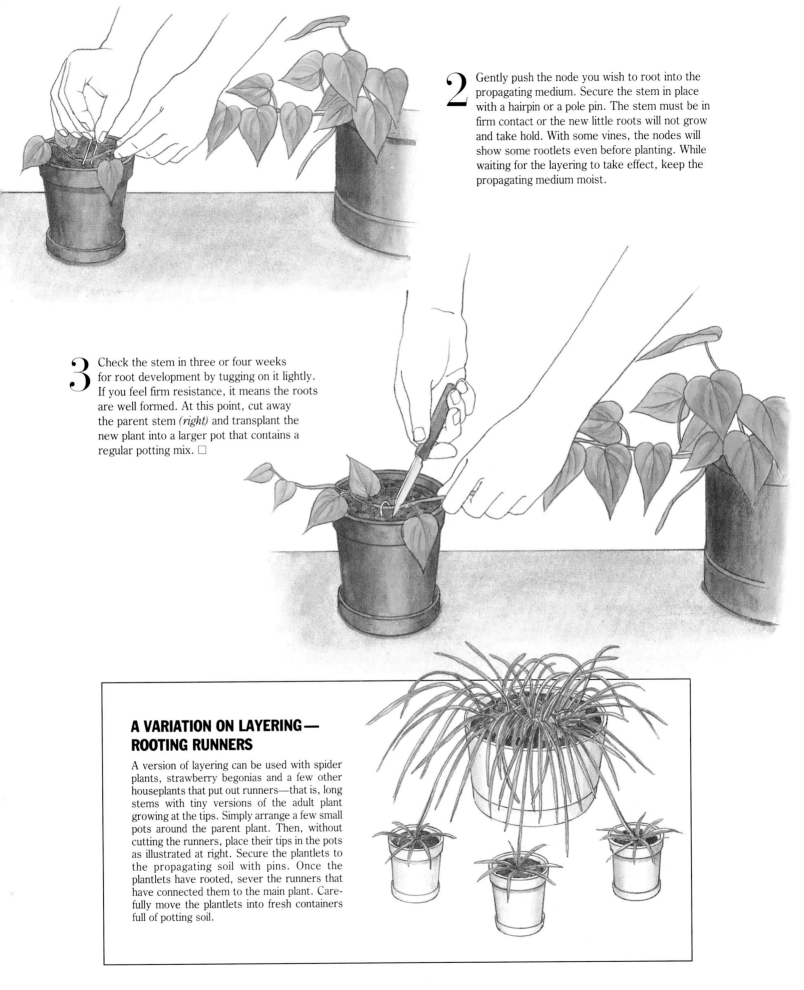

2 Gently push the node you wish to root into the propagating medium. Secure the stem in place with a hairpin or a pole pin. The stem must be in firm contact or the new little roots will not grow and take hold. With some vines, the nodes will show some rootlets even before planting. While waiting for the layering to take effect, keep the propagating medium moist.

3 Check the stem in three or four weeks for root development by tugging on it lightly. If you feel firm resistance, it means the roots are well formed. At this point, cut away the parent stem *(right)* and transplant the new plant into a larger pot that contains a regular potting mix. □

A VARIATION ON LAYERING— ROOTING RUNNERS

A version of layering can be used with spider plants, strawberry begonias and a few other houseplants that put out runners—that is, long stems with tiny versions of the adult plant growing at the tips. Simply arrange a few small pots around the parent plant. Then, without cutting the runners, place their tips in the pots as illustrated at right. Secure the plantlets to the propagating soil with pins. Once the plantlets have rooted, sever the runners that have connected them to the main plant. Carefully move the plantlets into fresh containers full of potting soil.

AIR LAYERING: NEW LIFE FOR A TALL PLANT

Propagating some of the more decorative and popular large houseplants—rubber trees, dumbcane and some types of fig— presents special difficulties. Cuttings taken from them seldom root well, and their stiff, woody stems cannot be bent over to permit a normal layering process *(page 48)*. The irony is that these plants cry out for some form of propagation. Growing tall, they often become oversized and look spindly, especially if they lose their lower leaves. The solution: new smaller editions—the sort of abbreviated versions that cuttings or layering might normally provide.

Enter a remarkable technique called air layering, a method of making plants grow new roots halfway up their stems—in midair, so to speak. The technique is an ancient one; it was evidently first used in China many centuries ago. This horticultural trick works admirably and is not particularly difficult to do.

The six steps involved in air layering are pictured at right and on the following two pages. In essence the method calls for making a cut into—but not through—the plant's stem. The cut is then encouraged to produce a fresh set of roots, helped along by some moist sphagnum moss, a bit of plastic wrap and a pinch of rooting hormone powder. When the roots have grown, the stem is severed and the top of the plant, with its new root system, is placed in a pot containing fresh soil. The result is a shorter and more shapely plant than the original spindly one, with fresh roots below—and a full growth of handsome foliage above. The parent plant will not only survive, but will also produce new foliage of its own from the remaining portion of the stem.

Displaying shiny, strong-veined foliage, a fiddle-leaf fig rises 4 feet above its basket-covered pot. Such treelike plants, which grow thick, woody stems, are ideally suited to propagation by the air-layering method.

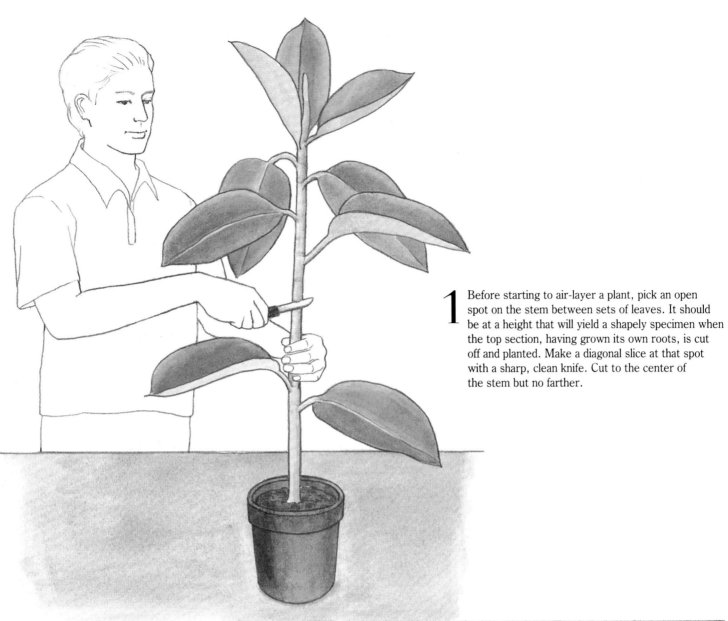

1 Before starting to air-layer a plant, pick an open spot on the stem between sets of leaves. It should be at a height that will yield a shapely specimen when the top section, having grown its own roots, is cut off and planted. Make a diagonal slice at that spot with a sharp, clean knife. Cut to the center of the stem but no farther.

2 Tap some rooting hormone powder onto a piece of paper, then dip the knife blade in it; some powder should adhere to the knife. Run the coated blade gently through the cut *(right),* leaving behind as much of the powder as possible. Repeat the application a couple of times to be sure that you have filled the opening with powder.

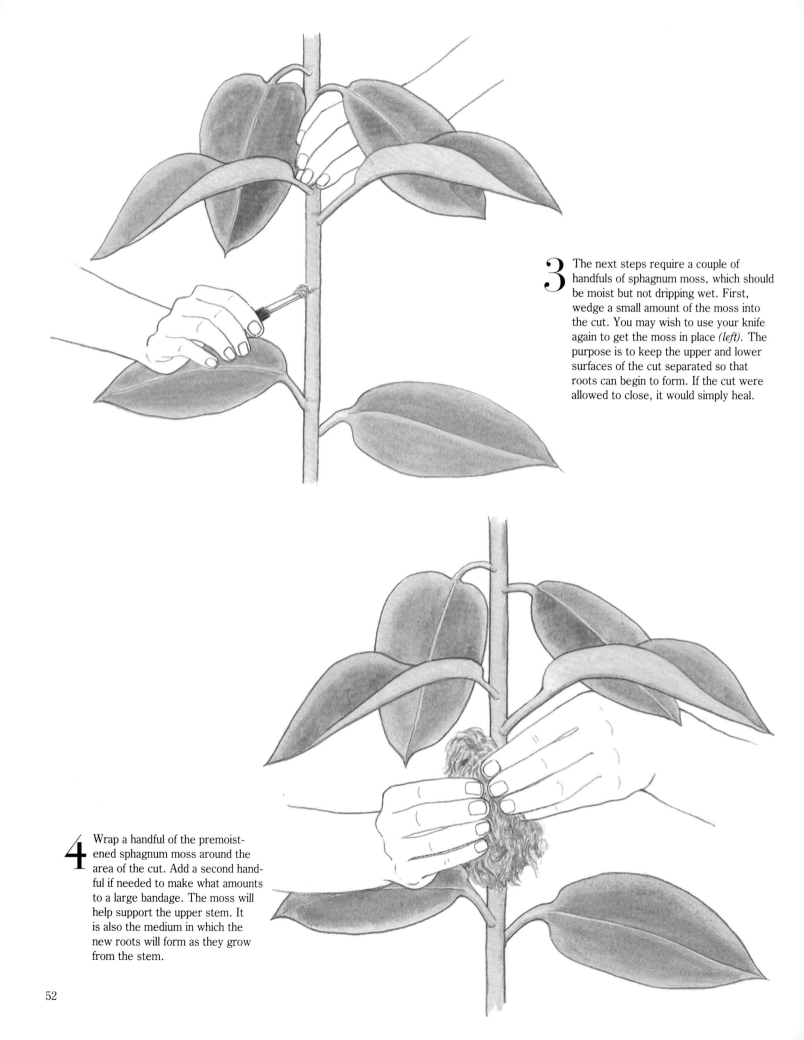

3 The next steps require a couple of handfuls of sphagnum moss, which should be moist but not dripping wet. First, wedge a small amount of the moss into the cut. You may wish to use your knife again to get the moss in place *(left)*. The purpose is to keep the upper and lower surfaces of the cut separated so that roots can begin to form. If the cut were allowed to close, it would simply heal.

4 Wrap a handful of the premoistened sphagnum moss around the area of the cut. Add a second handful if needed to make what amounts to a large bandage. The moss will help support the upper stem. It is also the medium in which the new roots will form as they grow from the stem.

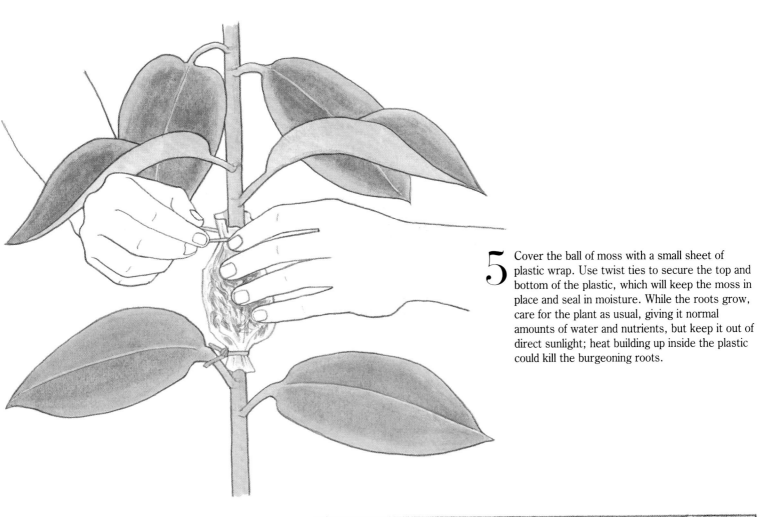

5 Cover the ball of moss with a small sheet of plastic wrap. Use twist ties to secure the top and bottom of the plastic, which will keep the moss in place and seal in moisture. While the roots grow, care for the plant as usual, giving it normal amounts of water and nutrients, but keep it out of direct sunlight; heat building up inside the plastic could kill the burgeoning roots.

6 After two or three months, a few new roots should be visible growing through the moss. When that has occurred, remove the plastic and sever the stem just below the new root ball *(right)*. Plant the rooted cutting in a soil-filled pot that is roomy enough but not too large *(page 8)*. Water well. Then cut back the stem of the parent plant to within a few inches of its soil line, to encourage the growth of fresh new leaves. □

DIVIDING ONE PLANT INTO MANY

Foliage houseplants that grow in clumps or develop from several growing points—asparagus fern, Boston fern, wandering Jew and others—can and should be propagated simply by being divided into several plants. Such rough treatment does not harm either the parent plant or its progeny. On the contrary, it benefits both.

The time to divide is the spring, when new growth is most vigorous. Prime candidates are plants that have become overgrown and pot-bound. Some plants, like the asparagus fern shown below and opposite, develop numerous swellings on their roots as they mature. The swellings themselves cause no harm, but their presence can cause pressure in the pot and the plant needs repotting to give them room. Usually, plants in this state display obvious signs of discomfort—yellowing, straggly foliage and a general air of weariness.

To break up a crowded plant, knock it gently from its pot and examine the roots. Look for places that will divide naturally. Some plants will break into a pair of clumps; others may produce four or more. Then pull the root ball apart with your fingers, making sure each clump has a cluster of leaves and a well-formed root system. A few plants have such densely interwoven roots that they will require cutting with a knife. When you have divided the clumps, put each in a separate pot of the proper size *(pages 8-9)*.

The whole process is anything but complex, and that goes for dividing other plants that produce what are called offsets—growths that spring spontaneously from the main stems and form small but identical new plants. For the best way to handle these, see the box at bottom right.

A Dallas fern spreads a green cascade of delicate fronds upward and outward from a simple, contrasting white pot. Like most ferns, this species grows fibrous roots that can be divided to produce more plants like itself.

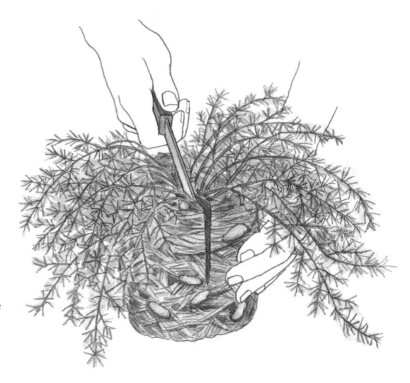

1 After taking your overgrown plant from its pot, determine how many clumps to break it into. Each division must have a clump of roots and a stem if it is to survive. If necessary, knock away or wash off some of the potting soil so that you can see the roots clearly. Then separate the sections by hand or with a sharp knife.

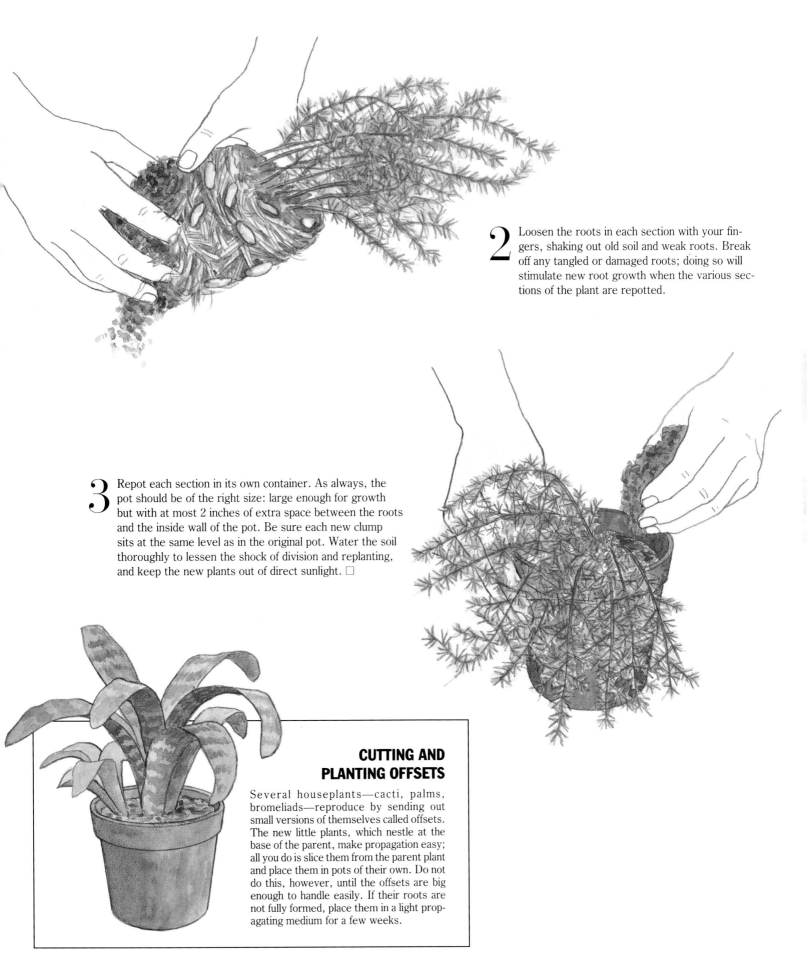

2 Loosen the roots in each section with your fingers, shaking out old soil and weak roots. Break off any tangled or damaged roots; doing so will stimulate new root growth when the various sections of the plant are repotted.

3 Repot each section in its own container. As always, the pot should be of the right size: large enough for growth but with at most 2 inches of extra space between the roots and the inside wall of the pot. Be sure each new clump sits at the same level as in the original pot. Water the soil thoroughly to lessen the shock of division and replanting, and keep the new plants out of direct sunlight. □

CUTTING AND PLANTING OFFSETS

Several houseplants—cacti, palms, bromeliads—reproduce by sending out small versions of themselves called offsets. The new little plants, which nestle at the base of the parent, make propagation easy; all you do is slice them from the parent plant and place them in pots of their own. Do not do this, however, until the offsets are big enough to handle easily. If their roots are not fully formed, place them in a light propagating medium for a few weeks.

RHIZOMES: STEMS THAT WILL ROOT

Some houseplants, including a number of ferns and rex begonias, have specialized stems, called rhizomes, that grow horizontally on or near the surface of the soil. Such plants can best be propagated from these curious structures. Rhizomes are often thick and fleshy—and sometimes hairy as well—and they tend to look more like roots than stems. But what rhizomes always have, and roots do not, are nodes—those little swellings found on all stems where leaves originate.

This is where propagation comes in. The nodes on rhizomes, in common with those on the stems of many plants, will root when pressed into some good propagating medium and, in time, will grow new plants. All that need be done, as seen in the drawings at right, is to find a good-sized rhizome on a mature fern or begonia, cut it off with a knife and put it in a pot.

Rhizomes are not hard to locate, for all their rootlike appearance. The leafstalks of begonias grow directly from them. The rhizomes on some ferns creep along the soil surface and look like the feet of furry animals—and so have given rise to the common names of such species as rabbit's-foot fern and squirrel's-foot fern. The larger the section of rhizome that is sliced off—2 inches is a minimum—the better chance it will include a vigorous rooting node.

The best season to propagate from rhizomes is the spring, when, like many other living things, they are primed to produce new growth. After a cut rhizome is started in its pot, it should sit in bright but filtered light. Then in three or four months, when the new plant is mature enough, it should be moved into a larger pot.

A pair of rabbit's-foot ferns, their long fronds as lacy and delicate as the curtain behind them, clearly display a half-dozen fuzzy, light brown rhizomes growing at soil level beneath the pale green foliage.

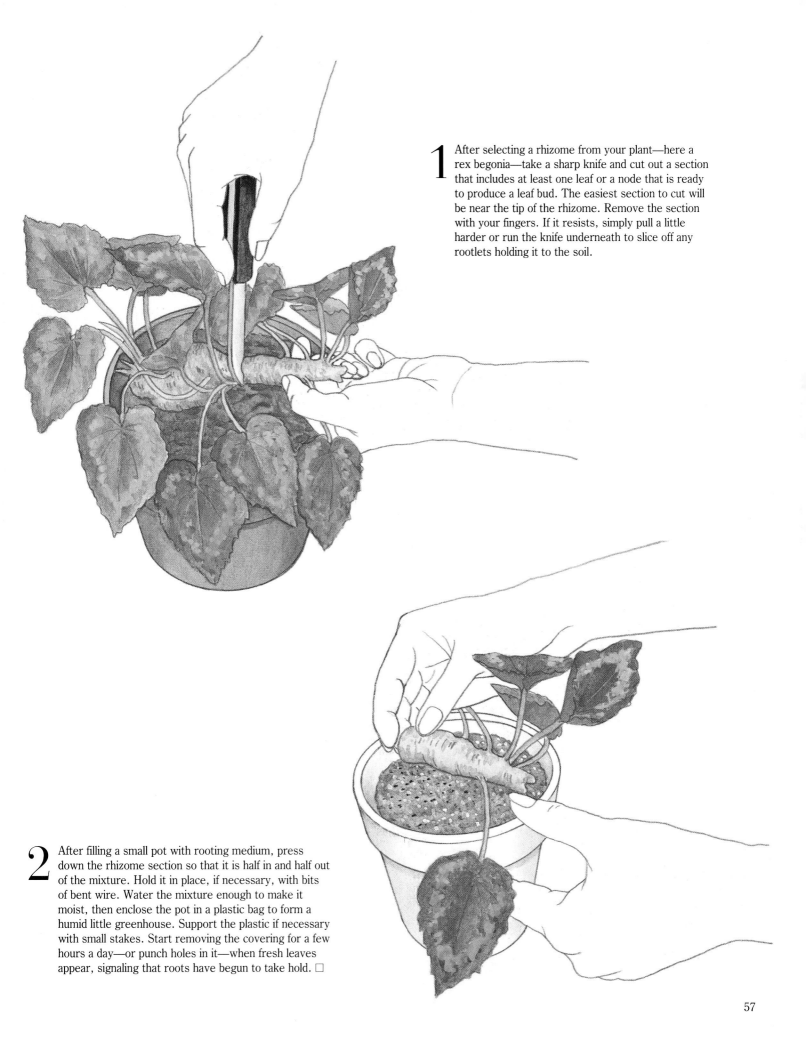

1 After selecting a rhizome from your plant—here a rex begonia—take a sharp knife and cut out a section that includes at least one leaf or a node that is ready to produce a leaf bud. The easiest section to cut will be near the tip of the rhizome. Remove the section with your fingers. If it resists, simply pull a little harder or run the knife underneath to slice off any rootlets holding it to the soil.

2 After filling a small pot with rooting medium, press down the rhizome section so that it is half in and half out of the mixture. Hold it in place, if necessary, with bits of bent wire. Water the mixture enough to make it moist, then enclose the pot in a plastic bag to form a humid little greenhouse. Support the plastic if necessary with small stakes. Start removing the covering for a few hours a day—or punch holes in it—when fresh leaves appear, signaling that roots have begun to take hold. □

A STRIKING HOUSEPLANT FROM A PINEAPPLE CROWN

T he crown of a pineapple—the top with the prickly leaves—is something that most people cut off and toss out with the garbage, since it isn't edible. But you can propagate an exotic houseplant from a pineapple crown, provided you start with one that is firm, fresh and undamaged. It should smell sweet but not heavy; heavily scented fruit is apt to be overripe. The pineapple crown should be still on the green side; overripe fruit may not have enough living tissue left to promote the development of new roots.

A properly prepared crown—scraped and air-dried to prevent rot, then set in a soilless medium of perlite and peat moss—should form roots within four to eight weeks. A sign of root formation is the emergence of new leaves from the center of the old foliage. Once roots are established, transplant the growing pineapple to a new pot.

Pineapples will grow best in a fast-draining, soil-based potting mix. Place the plant in a warm, sunny spot. Keep the soil just barely moist, and lightly mist the foliage every day or two.

Homegrown pineapple plants are raised for their striking foliage, not for edible fruit. But given ideal conditions—sufficient sun and humidity, temperatures in the 60° to 70° F range—your plant may produce a small pineapple after about three years.

A homegrown pineapple ripens on a mature plant that was started from the crown of a pineapple fruit. After harvesting, the crown of this pineapple can be dried and used to propagate yet another plant.

1 Lay a firm, green pineapple on its side. Using a clean, sharp knife, cut off the top of the pineapple about 1½ to 2 inches below the top of the crown *(right)*. If the spines on the top of the pineapple seem sharp, wear gloves to protect your hands.

2 To guard against rot, scrape as much soft pulp as possible from inside the crown with a fork or a knife. Be careful not to damage the hard core *(inset)* directly beneath the foliage, since this is where roots will form. Leave the outer skin intact.

3 Lay the crown on its side, out of direct sunlight, and let it dry for several days. In a large pot place a rooting medium of perlite and peat moss, and form a mound. Place the air-dried crown over the mound *(right)* and press down. Place the potted crown in indirect sunlight. Keep the medium evenly moist.

4 After a month, when the pineapple skin has withered, check for root development by tugging at the top; resistance means roots have formed. Gently remove the pineapple. Cut off whatever remains of the skin and transplant the pineapple to a larger pot *(left)* filled with a fast-draining all-purpose soil mix consisting of peat moss, potting soil, and sand or perlite. Keep the pineapple warm and moist. □

3
SHOWING OFF
YOUR HOUSEPLANTS

Houseplants, which are by nature decorative, tend to originate in some of the more out-of-the-way and unfriendly parts of the globe—in blazing deserts, sunless rain forests and steamy bogs. Perhaps these extreme conditions account in part for their exotic colorations and markings, their odd shapes and habits of growth—for the variegated leaves of caladium, the fuzzy leaves of the purple passion vine, the deeply cut leaves of the Swiss cheese plant, the curious fronds of the brake fern. Whatever the cause of such oddities, clearly the plants themselves are likely to respond more readily to the unfamiliar environment of the indoors if they are displayed in ways that exploit their natural habits of growth and that mimic their natural habitats.

On the following pages are instructions for creating suitable settings for a wide range of typical houseplants. Most of them use quite ordinary materials. There is, for example, a terrarium made from a cookie jar; its humid microclimate is just right for plants that originated in tropical rain forests. And, for an added bonus, it is practically self-perpetuating, since it almost never needs watering. At the opposite end of the spectrum is a dish garden that resembles a miniature desert, a fitting home for a cactus. Other specialized habitats include hanging baskets for trailing plants and a pseudobog for plants that take their nourishment from insects rather than the soil. There are instructions for mounting certain tropical airborne plants on driftwood and wreaths, and for caring for these plants, which normally take their nourishment in the air. Finally, for a decorative fillip, there are directions for arbitrarily training certain houseplants to grow into the shape of trees, with trunks and leafy tops, or to grow on wire forms that are miniature replicas of topiary hedges.

A TERRARIUM
FOR LOW CARE AND HIGH VISIBILITY

Four varied but compatible plants—a yellow-speckled croton, a prostrate silver-nerve plant, a tall satinwood and a variegated creeping fig—share the warm, moist microclimate inside a glass terrarium.

Nothing attracts attention and starts conversation like a terrarium—a glass-walled showcase in which a number of compatible plants can be displayed together. A terrarium is also almost maintenance-free; except for periodic pruning, plants in a terrarium require practically no care. That is because a terrarium, properly prepared for good drainage *(opposite and following pages),* provides a microclimate in which the plants thrive. It creates its own "weather," a self-regulating cycle of evaporation and precipitation. Moisture is absorbed from the soil by a plant's roots and passed on to the leaves, which release it into the air as water vapor; the vapor condenses on the inside of the glass and runs down into the soil, where it is absorbed by roots to begin the cycle anew. Containers made expressly for the purpose are available at garden centers and mail-order supply houses. Or you can make your own terrarium from a glass container such as a wide-mouthed cookie jar or a clean, dry aquarium tank. If you use an aquarium tank, you will need to fashion a removable top out of a pane of glass or a sheet of plastic.

When selecting plants for a terrarium, combine textures, shapes and sizes in a pleasing design as you would for an outdoor garden. There is a wide variety of material to choose from, since the highly humid conditions inside a terrarium resemble the steamy natural habitats of many houseplants. Good candidates include peperomia, table fern, Venus's hair, mosaic plant, purple waffle plant and creeping fig. About the only plants to be avoided are ones like cacti and succulents, which prefer a dry environment, and all large or quick-growing species that would soon become cramped in the limited space available.

1 To create the good drainage that is essential in a terrarium, pour ½ to 1 inch of some coarse material, like gravel, into the bottom of the container; this layer will collect excess water that would otherwise remain in the soil and cause the roots to rot. Buy presterilized gravel, or sterilize gravel with boiling water before using it.

2 Pour the same amount of sterile builder's sand on top of the gravel *(left)* and smooth it into an even layer with your hand. Besides providing additional drainage, the sand will prevent the soil above from sifting down into the gravel where it might become waterlogged.

3 On top of the sand, sprinkle about 1 tea-spoonful of activated charcoal *(right)*. With conditions inside the terrarium ideal for bacterial and fungal growth, the charcoal is needed to absorb any odors that may form.

4 Add at least 2 inches of potting soil *(right)*. Use a light mixture that holds moisture well, provides good aeration and is not too rich; you don't want to encourage your plants to outgrow the terrarium. The soil layer can be patted flat or sculpted into miniature hills and valleys.

5 Unpot the plants that you have selected for your terrarium and prepare them for transplanting. If a specimen looks too large to fit comfortably in the container, pull off the growth at the base of the stem *(left)*.

6 For each plant, poke a hole in the soil layer with your finger; then insert the plant so that it sits at the same depth in the terrarium as it sat in its original pot. Lightly firm the soil around the plant with your fingers. Finish putting in all your plants this way.

7 Add water to the terrarium; pour slowly and gently until you can see water seeping down to the sand layer. Do not add fertilizer; this would only stimulate unwanted growth.

8 Put the lid on the terrarium. Display it in indirect sunlight; too much sun might overheat the interior. If excessive condensation collects on the inside wall—enough to block your view of the plants—leave the lid off for a day or two to allow some of the trapped moisture to escape. You will rarely need to add water, but if the soil appears dry, wet it until water appears in the sand layer. And to keep the plants at the size you want, give them an occasional pruning. □

CREATING
A MINIATURE DESERT LANDSCAPE

Slow-growing, shallow-rooted, water-conserving cacti and succulents are ideal candidates for a special type of indoor environment known as a dish garden. These plants originated in arid regions of the world, and in the course of evolution, they modified their leaves (to reduce water loss through evaporation) and learned to store moisture in their swollen stems. Having adapted to survival on very little water, they will rot if they are kept in wet soil. They need to be planted in a container that facilitates fast drainage. A dish garden, created in a shallow container of unglazed clay or terra-cotta, which "breathes out" moisture, will do just that. Plastic containers, which tend to hold in moisture, should be avoided.

Making a desert-in-a-dish is a simple procedure. After selecting a container, you need only add a layer of drainage material—to help keep water away from the roots—and potting soil.

Although you may have room for only three or four plants, apply the same principles of scale and harmony in creating your miniature desert as you would in a full-scale landscape. Combine plants of different heights, shapes and colors but be sure to arrange them so that taller plants don't obscure shorter ones. To emphasize the desert motif, add a layer of white sand or small pebbles.

Place the finished dish garden in a sunny location. The only maintenance required is an occasional thorough watering—once a month in winter, slightly oftener the rest of the year. Let the soil dry between waterings.

Displayed together in a shallow dish, slow-growing cacti and succulents form a small-scale version of their native desert environment.

1 On the bottom of a shallow clay container, spread a ½-inch layer of gravel or similar coarse-textured drainage material. Fill the container to within 1 inch of the rim with a cactus mix *(page 10)*.

2 Exercise caution when you remove spiny cacti from their original pots. To guard your hands against scratches without damaging the plant, wrap several sheets of newspaper around the cactus and gently pull the plant from its pot *(right)*.

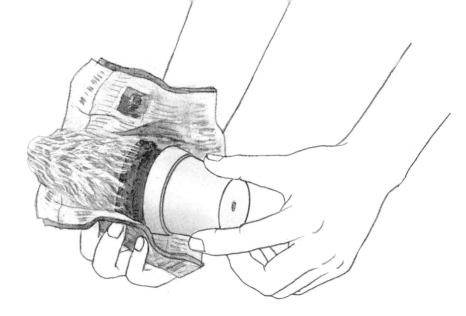

3 Dig a shallow hole in the soil. With your newspaper as protection for your hands, insert a cactus into the hole and situate it securely. Use a long stick or a spoon if necessary to firm the soil around the prickly perimeter of the plant.

4 After planting the rest of your cacti and succulents, water the soil thoroughly. Add decorative touches like pebbles or white builder's sand. Wait until the soil feels very dry before watering the plants again. □

TRAINING VINES IN ORNAMENTAL SHAPES

T he art of topiary—training trees and hedges to assume the shapes of animals and geometric designs —has challenged gardeners since early Roman times. Small wire frames that are available commercially in a variety of whimsical shapes (cats, dogs, ducks) make it possible for you to try your hand at topiary indoors. Instead of trees and hedges, indoor topiary makes use of easily trained stem cuttings from vines like the small-leaved ivies (English or Swedish) and creeping plants like creeping fig.

Buy a frame at a garden center or through a mail-order catalog. Estimate the number of cuttings it will take to cover the frame— usually one every 3 to 5 inches—and start propagating these as described on pages 36-39. When the rooted cuttings are 6 to 8 inches long, you can transplant them to the topiary figure. Soil mixed with a liberal quantity of sphagnum moss will fill out the hollow body of your topiary frame and provide a growing medium for the cuttings.

Don't expect a finished look immediately; it will take a while before the wire skeleton and moss stuffing are entirely hidden beneath dense foliage. To keep your topiary creation healthy and attractive in the meantime, make sure the sphagnum moss is always moist. Display the frame on a shallow tray; periodically fill the tray with water and let the moss soak up the moisture it needs. In addition, mist it daily, since the moss loses moisture rapidly. Every two weeks or so, pour a solution of water and water-soluble fertilizer over the topiary.

As the transplanted cuttings grow, continue to train them in the direction you want by winding their tips around the wire frame. To maintain a neat outline, prune stragglers as necessary.

This whimsical topiary pony, growing on a wire frame stuffed with moist sphagnum moss, sports a coat of creeping fig and a mane and tail of variegated spider plants. The eye is a shiny glass button.

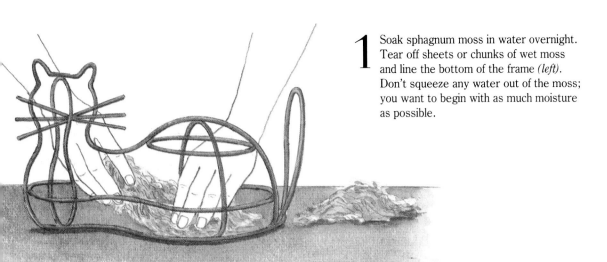

1 Soak sphagnum moss in water overnight. Tear off sheets or chunks of wet moss and line the bottom of the frame *(left)*. Don't squeeze any water out of the moss; you want to begin with as much moisture as possible.

2 Stuff the open cavity of the frame with a mixture of one part sphagnum moss and one part all-purpose potting soil *(right)*. This mixture will provide additional nourishment and stability to the roots of the cuttings.

3 Continue filling out the rest of the frame with wet moss. Where necessary, tie clear nylon fishing line between the wires to help hold the moss in place. Don't bother trying to fit moss into two-dimensional features like ears and tails.

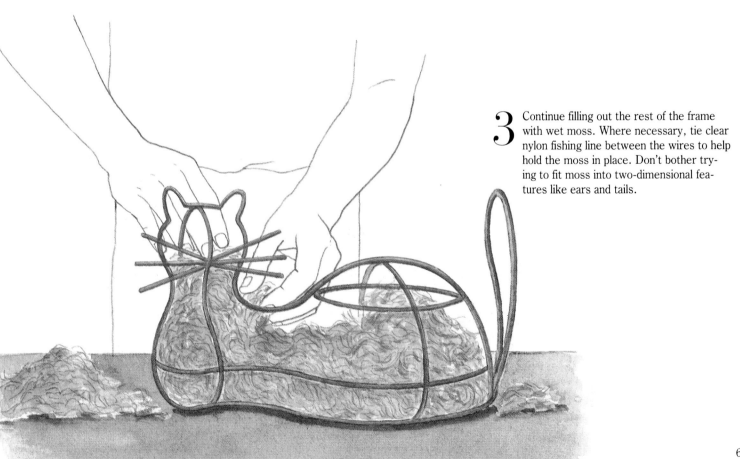

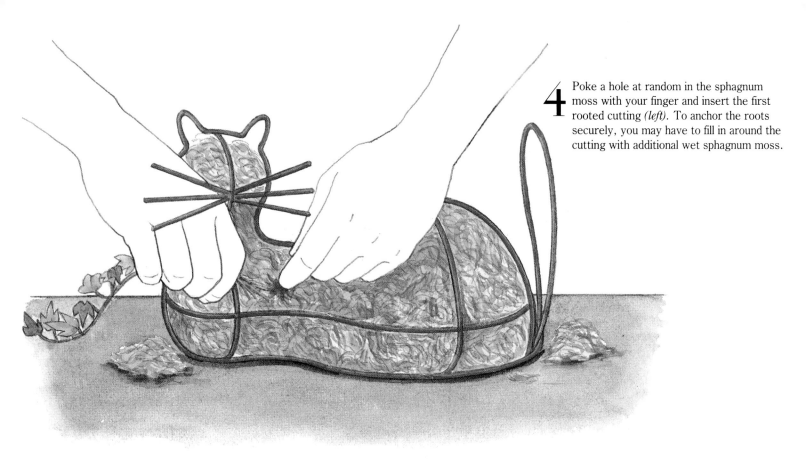

4 Poke a hole at random in the sphagnum moss with your finger and insert the first rooted cutting *(left)*. To anchor the roots securely, you may have to fill in around the cutting with additional wet sphagnum moss.

5 Begin training the cutting by draping the stem over the surface of the frame in the desired direction. Use plant pins—available at garden supply centers—to hold unruly stems in place. Transplant all your cuttings in this manner, spacing them out evenly across the frame.

6 To train a cutting to cover a two-dimensional feature such as a tail *(left)*, wrap a stem in ascending spiral fashion around the wire forming the tail. Secure it by weaving the tip of the stem under the loop at the top. Cover each ear in the same way.

7 Keep the completed topiary on a waterproof tray. At the first sign of dryness, fill the tray with water. When the moss has soaked up the water it needs, dispose of any excess remaining on the tray with a sponge or a syringe. Maintain the desired shape by training the plants as they grow—and by pruning any stray stems. □

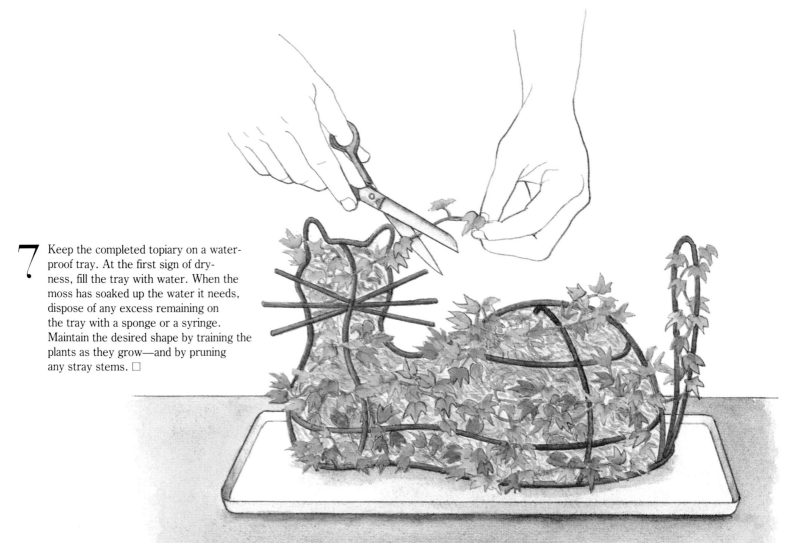

EXPANDING INDOOR GROWING SPACE WITH A HANGING GARDEN

When you need to find more room for your burgeoning houseplant collection, all you have to do is look up. Containers of carefully chosen plants suspended from walls and ceilings make eye-catching additions to any decor.

Because their environment differs, hanging plants have different growth requirements from their ground-level neighbors. The higher above the floor, the warmer the air, so hanging plants tend to dry out more quickly than those placed on a table or a windowsill. For this reason, the potting medium should be a light mixture of soil and humus so it will hold moisture. Also, plastic containers (which retain moisture) are preferable to containers made of porous clay.

You can hang containers from hooks embedded in the ceiling, or from wall brackets. Make sure you buy ones that are strong and that you fasten them securely, because containers filled with wet soil and plant material are surprisingly heavy.

When hanging your plants, choose a location that is a safe distance from the drying heat of a radiator. Beware of hanging your plants too high. Plants at eye level are not only attractive, they can be cared for without climbing ladders or taking down the containers. To facilitate watering, buy a can with a long narrow-nosed spout or a plastic squeeze bottle with a long flexible tube. Be sure your containers come with attached saucers to catch excess water.

Select plants with trailing or cascading habits, such as philodendron, Swedish ivy, wandering Jew, rosary vine and asparagus fern. If you want to grow several species in one container, make sure you choose plants that have similar light, soil and moisture requirements.

For a lush, bushy look, start with stem cuttings rather than commercially raised plants and periodically pinch off the tips of the stems. Avoid overcrowding; for example, five cuttings should be sufficient to fill out a container 8 inches in diameter.

Cascading from a white plastic hanging basket, the graceful foliage of a heart-leaf philodendron adds visual interest to a corner of a screened-in porch.

1 Fill a container with a potting mixture of light soil and humus to about 1 inch below the rim. Use a finger to dig a hole 1 inch to 2 inches from the wall of the container. Insert the rooted cutting and firm the soil around the base of the stem. Plant other cuttings about 1 to 2 inches apart.

2 Encourage the stems to put out fuller side growth by regularly pinching off the tips *(left)*. Pinch ¼ to ½ inch from the tip, preferably just above a node where a leaf attaches to the stem.

3 Water thoroughly. If the soil settles, add enough to bring the level back to 1 inch below the rim. Securely attach a hanger to the container and hang it in a safe place where routine maintenance is easy, and where it will not be subject to drafts or to heat. □

TROPICAL PLANTS THAT GROW WITHOUT SOIL

Epiphytes, or air plants, are plants that grow on any convenient perch they can find, like a tree trunk or a branch. Once anchored, they are able to satisfy all their needs without soil. They draw moisture from the air and gather nutrients from organic debris deposited by insects and falling leaves.

Many epiphytes are native to tropical rain forests, where very little sunlight reaches the ground. In an effort to get more sun, jungle trees grow tall. Air plants, which also need sun, obtain it by attaching themselves to the treetops, sometimes at great heights off the ground.

With a little ingenuity, you can encourage a fascinating collection of epiphytes to grow on a natural-looking perch of your own choosing, such as a piece of driftwood or bark or (as illustrated here) a wreath made of grapevines stripped of their leaves. Besides the perch, all you need is a little sphagnum moss to help anchor the roots and keep them moist. Among the air plants that do quite well at home are the staghorn fern and the bromeliads. Most bromeliads are air plants, although the best-known member of the family—the common pineapple—is not.

Bromeliads capable of living in air have shallow roots that serve primarily as anchors; the leaves, in spite of their stiff, leathery appearance, are adapted to take in water directly. In many varieties a rosette of leaves grows in such a way as to form a central "cup" at the base of the plant. The plant takes in nourishment and water through this cup.

Plants that thrive as epiphytes can also be grown in a soilless potting mix. But they do best under conditions that mimic the upper levels of a tropical rain forest: suspended from a secure perch in a sunny, humid location. If the plant has a cup, keep it filled with water at all times. Mist it regularly, making sure that both leaves and roots are thoroughly moistened.

An earth-star, a Medusa's head and a neoregelia —three bromeliads that are also air plants—are cradled in damp sphagnum moss and secured to a piece of driftwood by thin fishing line.

1 Unpot your air plants and arrange them on the surface of the perch you have chosen (a wreath made of grapevines is illustrated here). Move the plants around until you find a design you like.

2 To mount the plants on the wreath, wrap a handful of wet sphagnum moss around each root ball. Tie one end of cotton twine or nylon fishing line to the wreath, loop the twine two or three times around the root ball, then tie the free end to the wreath. If the plant seems loose, stuff extra moss under the twine until it no longer wobbles.

3 After mounting all your plants, water them. If they are bromeliads that have hollow cuplike depressions at their bases, pour water directly into the cups *(right);* otherwise mist the plants and the moss around them. Hang the finished wreath on the wall. Maintain moisture by watering (or misting) the plants regularly. □

A BOG
FOR CARNIVOROUS PLANTS

In a "bog" of sphagnum moss, a Venus flytrap with its pouchlike tops and two varieties of sundew with sticky hairs on their long slender stalks stand ready to catch small insects to feed on.

Carnivorous plants are among nature's evolutionary wonders. They are native to the wetlands, where soil is deficient in the decomposed animal and vegetable matter that supplies key nutrients like nitrogen. To survive, these plants must supplement their mineral-poor diet with fresh food.

The Venus flytrap, for example, which comes from the bogs of the Carolinas, has modified its leaves into lethal weapons. The leaves secrete a nectar whose smell attracts insects. Sensitive hairs act as trip wires; when touched, they trigger a mechanism that snaps the leaf shut. Spikelike "teeth" around the rim of the leaf mesh together, locking in the unwary intruder whose body is then slowly digested by special enzymes.

As exotic as these plants appear, they are easy to grow at home if you provide boggy conditions that resemble their native habitat: high humidity, sunlight, an acidic, well-aerated growing medium. An open terrarium vessel (like a large fishbowl) packed with sphagnum moss is ideal.

You can purchase dry sphagnum moss at any garden supply center. Ask for unmilled moss with the long strands intact; milled sphagnum moss deteriorates too quickly. Even better—if you can find it—is live, green sphagnum moss; some mail-order houses that specialize in terrariums and carnivorous plants sell it.

Once your miniature bog is set up, maintenance is minimal. Keep it in a sunny location. Change the moss when it deteriorates. Maintain an even moisture level. And if the plants catch insects, no fertilizer is needed.

1 On the bottom of your container, spread about 1 inch of drainage material such as sterile gravel. Cover that with a light layer of sand. On top of the sand add a thick layer—3 to 6 inches, depending on the size of the container—of pre-moistened sphagnum moss *(left)*. To ensure good aeration, do not pack the moss down.

2 Poke a hole in the sphagnum moss with your fingers. Gently remove a plant from its old pot and place it in the hole *(above)*. Work the moss lightly around the plant to hold it upright. Insert the rest of the plants in this manner, with an eye toward creating an interesting design.

3 Gently pour in water until it starts to collect in the drainage layer *(left)*. To maintain the constantly wet environment that carnivorous plants like, add more water whenever the tips of the moss dry out and lighten in color. Replace moss as it starts to disintegrate. If the plants don't consume insects, you can add a small amount of diluted fertilizer to the water once a week. □

STANDARDS—
PLANTS THAT LOOK LIKE TREES

The stems of three fig saplings intertwine to form the decorative "trunk" of this braided standard. The tree-like crown was created by selective pruning.

A standard is a plant that would ordinarily grow in a spreading form, but has been trained to look like a tree; it has a dense, compact crown of foliage atop a bare trunklike stem. An interesting variation *(opposite and following pages)* is known as a braided standard. The stems of three or more individual plants are interwoven to form a composite "trunk." Either way, with its neat, rather formal appearance, a standard makes a handsome addition to any indoor garden.

Creating a standard involves little more than diligent pruning and pinching. Among the plants that respond well to this treatment are weeping fig, geraniums and ming aralia; over time they all develop thick stems that will support a large top growth. If the standard is braided, the stems may eventually fuse to form a trunk with a decoratively gnarled appearance.

For a single standard, start with a young plant that has a strong central stem; for a braided standard, use rooted stem cuttings. To encourage the formation of a trunk, prune away all side growth from the base of the stem or stems when you begin the standard, and then prune repeatedly as the plant grows. To promote a full crown, pinch the top growth selectively. Pinch or clip off stems that emerge from the sides of the crown, but leave the uppermost tip of the central stem of each plant intact. This tip, known as the terminal growing point, will guide the plant's vertical development. Remove it only when the plant has reached the desired height—which may take several years with a weeping fig.

Because of their top-heavy foliage, most standards must be supported on stakes. This can be done at the first pruning. Soft-stemmed plants like geraniums and coleus require permanent staking; woodier plants like weeping fig and ming aralia may be able to stand on their own once they have matured.

To make a braided standard, as shown opposite and on the following pages, only rooted stem cuttings should be used. They must be firm enough to be established, but young enough to be pliable. For easy reference, the three stems in the illustrations are labeled *A, B* and *C*. The main point to remember in braiding is that an outer strand is always moved to the central position. In choosing the outer strands to move, alternate between left and right.

1 To start a braided fig, fill a pot with soil and, in the center, plant three rooted stem cuttings about 1 inch apart from one another. The cuttings should be 12 to 18 inches long. With clean, sharp pruning shears, remove all lower leaves and any forking branches *(right)*. To prevent protruding stubs, always cut flush with the main stem. Leave the top growth intact.

2 To begin the braid, take hold of the center stem (labeled *B* and colored yellow in the inset) with one hand and hold it steady; grasp stem *A* (colored red) with the other hand, and cross one over the other so that *A* moves to the center.

A   B   C

A   B   C

3 Keeping hold of stem *A* with one hand, grasp stem *C* (colored blue) with the other hand and carry it across *A* so that stem *C* takes the central position.

79

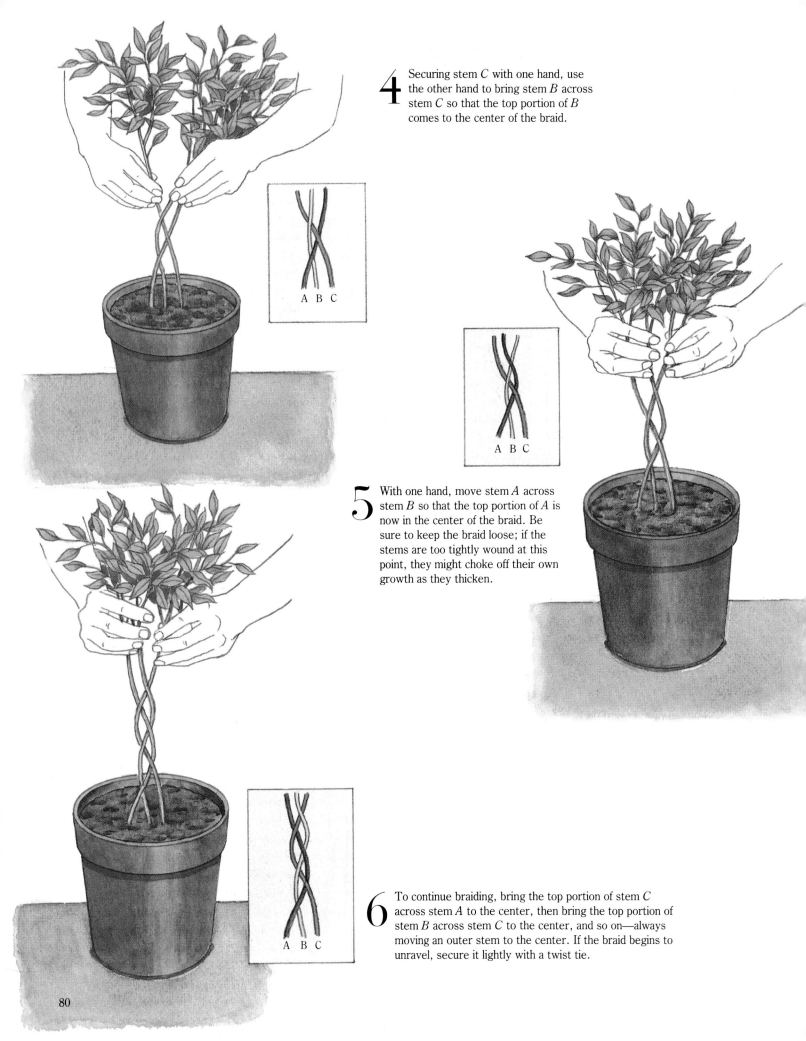

4 Securing stem C with one hand, use the other hand to bring stem B across stem C so that the top portion of B comes to the center of the braid.

A B C

5 With one hand, move stem A across stem B so that the top portion of A is now in the center of the braid. Be sure to keep the braid loose; if the stems are too tightly wound at this point, they might choke off their own growth as they thicken.

A B C

6 To continue braiding, bring the top portion of stem C across stem A to the center, then bring the top portion of stem B across stem C to the center, and so on—always moving an outer stem to the center. If the braid begins to unravel, secure it lightly with a twist tie.

A B C

7 Encourage a dense treelike crown by pinching off stems that emerge from the sides *(left),* but take care not to disturb the terminal growing point that directs the upward growth of each of the three plants you started with. Keep braiding and pinching as the plant grows. Remove side growth from the lower "trunk" as soon as it appears.

8 At some point in its development, a braided fig may become top-heavy. To keep it upright, insert a stake in the soil close to the plant and attach it to the "trunk" with twist ties or some string. Remove the stake when the braided stems are sturdy enough to bear the weight of the crown.

9 Once the plant has reached the height you want, remove the terminal growing points with shears *(left).* From now on, instead of growing taller, the plant will concentrate on sending out side growth. Prune as necessary. □

PROGRAM FOR SUMMER: OUTDOOR AIR AND SUNLIGHT

Indoor gardeners who live in regions where warm spring weather is predictable and summers are hot should give their houseplants outdoor vacations. Most indoor favorites thrive on sunlight, rain and fresh air. A few species —those with soft, fuzzy leaves, such as purple passion vine—are best left indoors. But the rest can be moved outdoors, pots and all, as soon as spring has arrived—when night temperatures no longer dip below 50° F. And they can stay out at least until early autumn.

The plants in their pots can be arranged along the edge of a porch or a patio, but a better method is to sink the containers in the ground, as shown below and at right. The earth insulates the plants from abrupt temperature changes and helps keep the pots and their contents from drying out.

Naturally, pampered indoor plants need to be acclimated to outdoor life. Start by placing the pots in a shady, wind-protected corner for a couple of hours each day for a week, then lengthen the time outdoors gradually for another week. Once they are settled full-time on a patio or in the garden, the plants should be fertilized as needed and watered liberally. Wind and sun speed moisture loss.

In the fall, begin reacclimating the plants for the move indoors by returning them to a shady, protected spot. Clean the pots thoroughly and inspect them for pests and diseases. To be safe, treat the plants with an insecticide, and quarantine the vacationers for a month so they cannot infect plants that have remained inside.

Two sorts of houseplants, green-and-white-leaved dumbcane and pink-and-green caladium, share a protected corner with its permanent residents, a fragrant daphne, a blooming azalea and a weeping cherry. Both indoor species thrive outdoors in warm weather if their pots are set in an area of dappled sunlight.

1 Before selecting an outdoor site, check the sun tolerance of each plant in the dictionary on pages 96-135. After choosing a spot that receives the right amount of light, dig a hole as wide as the pot and about 2 inches deeper.

2 Fill the bottom 2 inches of the hole with gravel. This will ensure good drainage—and be helpful in the fall when you pull up the pot to move it back indoors. As houseplants grow outdoors during the summer, their roots tend to reach through the pot's drainage hole and into the earth. The gravel layer helps keep the roots from spreading and makes it easier to dislodge them.

3 Place the potted plant in the hole. About ½ to 1 inch of the pot's rim should be above ground, to mark its location. Pour some of the dug-up earth around the pot and firm it with your hands. Spread a mulch in the area, to help conserve ground moisture.

4 Every two weeks or so, grasp the pot by its rim and give it a quarter turn. This rotation helps discourage the roots from locking too firmly into the gravel and soil below the pot. It also gives all the foliage even exposure to sunlight as the spring and summer progress. □

4
MAKING THE MOST OF NATURE

Even indoors, plants respond to seasonal changes. The same windowsill dweller that asks for infrequent watering and no fertilizer during the winter may develop a tremendous thirst and a voracious appetite once spring rouses it from winter languor. For every gardening task—potting and repotting, propagation and division, cleaning and pruning—there is a proper season. To find out what you should do and when to do it, turn to the year-round maintenance guide *(pages 86-87)*.

While houseplants adapt readily to different environments, most suffer when exposed to extremes of light, temperature and humidity. And even in the best of circumstances plants can fall prey to natural enemies like insect pests (which can enter your home through open windows) and disease-causing fungi and bacteria. The quicker you recognize the signs of distress, the quicker you can correct the problem. For a comprehensive, conveniently organized list of common houseplant problems— and effective remedies—look under the heading "What to Do When Things Go Wrong" *(pages 88-91)*.

Finally, there is a section of useful tips that will help you get the most out of your houseplants *(pages 92-95)*. You will learn how to give a plant a shower (don't forget the soap), how to pack up your plants when you move (lots of newspaper and foil), how to discourage cats and dogs from snacking on succulent greenery (mist the leaves with a tingly but harmless solution of water and cayenne pepper).

A GUIDE TO MAINTENANCE
SEASON BY SEASON

WINTER

- When days are short and light is low, plant growth slows, and the need for moisture and nutrients is reduced. Water your houseplants infrequently and apply little or no fertilizer.

- Cold drafts threaten plants on a windowsill and may cause loss of foliage. For nighttime protection, place a barrier such as a piece of cardboard between the plants and the window.

- Heating systems dry the air. Group your houseplants close together so they share the moisture released from foliage, or grow them on pebble trays to provide them with humidity.

- Spider mites are especially active in a warm, dry environment. Inspect your houseplants for signs of these and other insects and for diseases.

- Clean empty pots and prepare a potting medium for spring transplanting.

- Order seeds for spring sowing.

SPRING

- When days lengthen and light increases, houseplants resume active growth. Start to water and fertilize your houseplants regularly.

- Now is the time to propagate: sow seeds, take stem and leaf cuttings, layer and divide plants.

- When seedlings become large enough, transplant them to individual containers.

- Check the root systems of all houseplants and repot those that are pot-bound.

- Prune and pinch back leafy green plants to encourage full growth.

- Inspect all plants regularly for insects and diseases.

SUMMER

- Continue to water and fertilize your houseplants regularly.

- Check plants located near windows for signs of sunburn. If the leaves develop tan or brown patches between the veins, move the plants farther away from the source of light.

- Check plants that are not growing well to see if they are pot-bound and need to be repotted.

- Houseplants may be moved outdoors for the summer. Check them frequently; once the plants are outdoors, their growth increases, so they require more water and fertilizer.

- Transplant stem and leaf cuttings taken in spring to individual pots.

- Inspect all houseplants regularly for insects and diseases. Examine houseplants that you have put outdoors; look for damage done by snails, slugs and other garden pests.

FALL

- Prepare to return houseplants indoors. Wash the pots and the foliage to rinse off garden bacteria and insects. Bring the plants indoors as soon as night temperatures drop to 50° F.

- Take stem cuttings of tender perennials such as coleus, geraniums and iresine from the garden to be rooted and grown indoors as houseplants.

- As days shorten, light decreases and plant growth slows, reduce watering and fertilizing.

- As the weather cools and you turn on the heat, make sure your houseplants are grouped close together or placed on pebble trays for adequate humidity.

- Watch your houseplants for signs of insects and diseases, especially those that are active in a warm, dry environment.

WHAT TO DO WHEN THINGS GO WRONG

PROBLEM	CAUSE	SOLUTION
Leaves lose their color and may curl up. Leaves and stems may be covered with a shiny, sticky substance.	Aphids, ⅛-inch semitransparent insects that suck the sap from the foliage. Aphids secrete the sticky substance, which becomes a breeding ground for diseases.	Pick aphids off the plant by hand and destroy them. Wash the plant with lukewarm, soapy water and rinse well. If the infestation is severe, use an insecticide.
Foliage turns yellow and has a curled or puckered appearance. Brown or silver flecks or streaks may appear along the leaf veins.	Thrips, ¹⁄₁₆-inch, yellow, green or black insects barely visible to the naked eye. They suck the sap from the foliage.	Remove damaged leaves. Treat the plant with an insecticide.
Plants wilt, cease to grow and may die. White, cottonlike masses form at or just below the soil surface. Cacti and succulents are particularly susceptible.	Root mealybugs, ¹⁄₁₆-inch-long insects. Most species feed only on underground roots, but a few also feed on stems.	Dip the entire plant, including the pot, into an insecticide solution.
Plant growth slows or stops. Small, flying insects are evident in the area where plants are grown.	Fungus gnats, black flies up to ⅛ inch long. The flies do not feed on the plants, but they can spread diseases. The larvae, which hatch in the soil, may feed on plant roots.	Rinse the soil of infested plants with an insecticide. Use a household insect spray in the areas around the plants.
Plants cease to grow, and foliage turns yellow and then drops. When a plant is shaken or moved, a white cloud of insects appears above the foliage.	Whiteflies, ¹⁄₁₆-inch insects that congregate in colonies on the undersides of leaves and suck the sap from the foliage.	Wash the plant with lukewarm, soapy water and rinse well. If the infestation is severe, use an insecticide.
Patches of white, cottonlike growths appear on the undersides of leaves and at the points where the leaves join the stems. Foliage may be coated with a shiny, sticky substance. The plant ceases to grow and may die.	Mealybugs, ¼-inch insects that have soft round bodies covered with fuzzy white filaments. They suck the sap from the foliage and secrete the shiny substance, which becomes a breeding ground for diseases.	Moisten a cotton swab with alcohol and dab it on the mealybugs, which will die and fall off the plant. Then wash the plant in lukewarm, soapy water and rinse well. If the infestation is severe, use an insecticide.

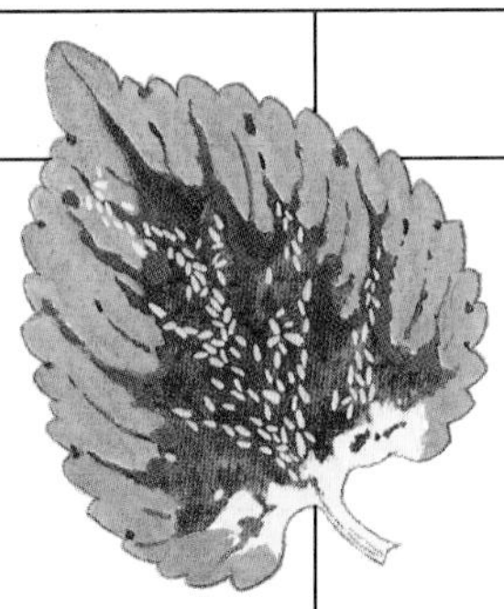

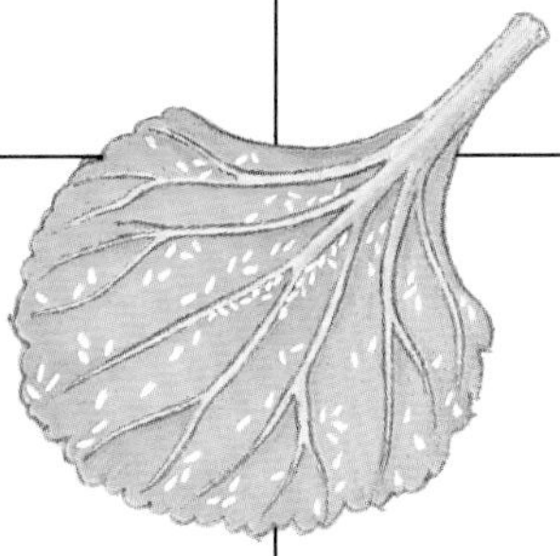

PROBLEM	CAUSE	SOLUTION
Foliage turns yellow and has a bronzy, dull appearance. Leaves may dry up and fall from the plant. Eventually, webbing will appear on the foliage.	Spider mites, nearly microscopic pests that may be red, yellow, green or black. To confirm their presence, gently shake a leafstalk over a piece of paper; tiny, moving, dustlike specks will appear on the paper.	Wash plants regularly with lukewarm water to prevent and control infestation. Maintain high humidity; mites thrive in hot, dry air. If the infestation is severe, use a miticide.
Small, irregular holes appear in leaves near the soil. After the plant is watered or moved, masses of small, rapidly moving insects become visible on the soil surface.	Springtails, white or gray wingless insects $\frac{1}{5}$ inch long that live in moist soil. Generally, they cause little damage, but when they are present in large numbers, some insects may feed on the foliage.	To prevent infestation, use a sterile medium for potting and allow the medium to dry between waterings. To control springtails, use an insecticide.
Foliage turns yellow and dies back. Rounded or oval bumps that are green, gray or brown appear along the stems and under the leaves. A shiny, sticky substance may cover the leaves.	Scale, a $\frac{1}{8}$-inch insect with a round or oval shell-like covering. Scale insects suck the sap from the foliage and secrete the sticky substance, which becomes a breeding ground for diseases.	Use lukewarm, soapy water and a soft brush to remove scales from the leaves; then rinse well. Treat severe infestations with an insecticide.
Brown patches appear at the bases of the fronds on bird's nest fern. The patches expand to cover the fronds and eventually the fronds die back.	Foliar nematodes, microscopic worms that bore into the fronds through the surface pores and then feed on the foliage.	There are no controls for nematodes. Allow the soil to dry between waterings. Do not splash water on the foliage; nematodes are spread by water. Cut off and destroy infested fronds. If damage is extensive, the plant and the potting soil should be discarded.
Plants become leggy and foliage is small and sparse. Leaves that should be variegated or colored red, pink or orange are solid green.	If the plant grows toward its light source, the cause is insufficient light. If the plant grows straight, but the leaves lose their variegation, the cause is usually excess fertilizer. The nitrogen in fertilizer speeds the growth of green cells, which overtake the colored cells.	Gradually move the plant into an area that receives more light or add fluorescent light. Reduce the amount of fertilizer. Cut the foliage back to encourage new growth.
Ferns turn yellow, beginning with the fronds in the center of the plant. The tips of the fronds turn brown. Eventually, entire fronds turn brown and die.	Low humidity.	Most ferns require high humidity. Move ferns to a humid location, place a humidifier nearby or grow ferns on a tray of moist pebbles *(page 20)*.

PROBLEM	CAUSE	SOLUTION
Leaves do not develop to their full size. They have a pale, faded color, and may wilt. Leaf edges become dry and brittle, but do not turn brown.	Insufficient water.	Water plants as soon as symptoms appear. If the soil has completely dried out, soak the pot in water for several hours until the entire root ball is moistened.
Leaf edges turn yellow. Yellowing spreads toward the center of leaf until the entire leaf is yellow and drops from the plant. Plant growth may be stunted.	Lack of nitrogen.	Cut the foliage back and begin fertilizing regularly. If symptoms persist, increase the amount of fertilizer.
Silvery white, tan or brown areas develop on leaves between the veins. Plant growth is extremely compact.	Excess light.	Remove damaged leaves and move the plant to an area that receives less light.
Leaves, especially those at the base of the plant, turn light green or yellow and may wilt. Roots become soft, turn brown or black, and may have an unpleasant, sour odor.	Too much water.	Prune back damaged plants and repot them in a fast-draining medium. Allow the soil to dry moderately between waterings.
Plants fail to grow. Leaves at the base of plants may turn yellow, wilt and die. Stems may be brown at the soil line. Roots are brown and soft.	Crown, root and stem rot caused by fungi that thrive in wet soils.	Allow the soil to dry between waterings. If the soil is heavy, repot the plant in a fast-draining, sterile soil mix.
Leaves become mottled or streaked with yellow. Plant growth slows.	Viral infection, a condition that may subside on its own.	There are no controls for viral infection, but it can be spread by aphids and other insects, which should be controlled (page 88). Infected plants should be isolated from healthy ones, and if the damage is severe, plants should be discarded.

90

PROBLEM	CAUSE	SOLUTION
Leathery brown or black patches appear on cacti. The patches enlarge and the areas eventually shrivel and die.	A condition called scab. The cause is unknown, but scab occurs primarily when cacti are kept in areas with high humidity and low light, and it seems to spread from cactus to cactus.	There are no controls. Provide cacti with bright light, dry air and dry soil. Discard infected plants.
Soft, sunken, brown or yellow areas appear on stems. Leaves below the diseased area will turn yellow, but will not drop from the plant. Eventually, stems may rot completely and collapse.	Bacterial stem blight, also called soft rot, a disease caused by bacteria that enter the plant through wounds in the stem.	There are no controls. Damaged stems may be removed with a sharp knife. If the damage is extensive, the plant should be discarded.
A fine white powder coats the upper surfaces of leaves and the stems. Foliage may dry out and drop from the plant.	Powdery mildew, a fungus disease. The fungus thrives in a combination of wet soil and stagnant air.	Keep houseplants in an area with good air circulation and allow the soil to dry between waterings. Wash mildew off plants with lukewarm, soapy water. In severe cases, treat the plant with a fungicide.
Leaf edges turn brown and brittle. Symptoms appear first on older leaves, which eventually turn yellow and die. White streaks or patches appear on the rims and exteriors of clay pots.	Salt buildup, caused by an excess of soluble salts in water, fertilizers or soil.	Leach salts that have built up in the soil by flushing the soil with fresh water several times; repeat until the water that drains out is clear. Empty saucers so plants do not stand in drainage water. If damage is severe, repot the plant in a fresh, sterile soil mix.
Brown spots appear on the stems of palm fronds. Eventually, the entire frond turns brown. A pink-brown mold may appear at the base of the stems.	Gliocladium rot, a fungal disease.	Remove any diseased fronds. Avoid splashing water on the fronds; the disease spreads in water. Treat infected palms with a fungicide.
Clusters of small green bumps or blisters appear on the surfaces of leaves. Eventually, the blisters turn brown. The leaves may turn yellow and drop.	Edema, a condition that results from excess water in the leaf cells, which causes them to blister.	There are no controls. Grow plants in fast-draining soil, and allow the soil to dry between waterings.
Red, brown or black spots appear on leaves; each spot may be surrounded by a yellow halo. The spots enlarge until they cover the leaves and eventually the leaves die.	Leaf spot disease, caused by bacteria or fungi.	There are no controls. Remove infected leaves. Do not allow water to splash on the foliage; the disease is spread by water.

TIPS AND TECHNIQUES

USING DECORATIVE CONTAINERS

Ceramic, brass, rattan and straw containers are popular choices for displaying houseplants, but they are often made without drainage holes. Since poor drainage can cause the planting medium to become waterlogged and disease-prone, such containers should not used for planting. Instead, plants should be grown in pots with drainage holes, and these pots can be placed in decorative containers.

By keeping a pot within a pot, excess water that collects in the outside container can be drained off. If a plant is too large to lift in order to empty excess water, a layer of peat moss or vermiculite can be placed between the two pots. These materials absorb excess water so the bottom of the plant is not resting in water.

Containers of rattan and straw eventually disintegrate if they are subject to moisture. To prevent this, line these containers with plastic before inserting pots in them.

GROWING HOUSEPLANTS WITHOUT SOIL

A simple way to fill your house with leafy green plants is to cut a stem from a plant and stick it in a container of water, where the cutting will develop its own root system. There are several plants that readily adapt to life in the water, and they include arrowhead vine, Chinese evergreen, dracaena, dumbcane, ivy and philodendron. The main advantage of growing plants in water is ease of maintenance. Once you've placed your cutting in water, it needs little attention. The water should be changed weekly, and a water-soluble fertilizer should be added to the water about once a month.

Generally, plants that have rooted in water will not grow well if they are transplanted into soil, so they should be kept in water even when they mature. For an attractive display, use colored bottles or clear bottles with colored pebbles added.

BRINGING PLANTS INTO YOUR HOME

Most of the houseplants you buy at a store or garden center are recent transfers from the ideal conditions of a commercial greenhouse. These plants will eventually adapt to the lower light levels and lower humidity of the home, and you can help them make the transition.

The best times to bring new plants into the home are in spring and summer, when light levels are higher than in winter. But whatever time of year you bring new plants home, place them where they will receive lots of light. If a plant's permanent location will be in limited light, begin moving the plant away from bright light over a period of days. The gradual move will allow the plant to adjust to the lower light level.

GREEN AND GLOWING LEAVES

Clean, shiny foliage is not only attractive; it is also a sign of good health. When dust and dirt are allowed to accumulate on foliage, they can clog leaf pores and prevent adequate light from reaching leaf surfaces, which causes poor leaf color and plant growth.

To keep your plants at their best, clean the foliage regularly. If your plants are small enough, take them into your bathroom once a month and give them a shower. Not only does the stream of water clean the leaves, it also rinses away small insects. If your plants are too large to move, you can sponge the leaves with lukewarm, soapy water and then wipe them clean with clear water. Be sure the foliage is dry before moving the plant back into sunlight. If the leaves of your plants are too small to be sponged off, they can be dusted with a feather duster.

Do not coat the leaves with any substance containing oil; oil can clog leaf pores and keep the plants from respiring properly.

TREATING SALT BUILDUP

If salts accumulate on the rims and sides of your pots, they may threaten healthy foliage; salts can cause leaf edges to turn brown. But pots covered with white, filmy salt patches don't need to be discarded; they just need a thorough cleaning.

After removing your plants from the pots, use a stiff brush to scrub off crusted salts and dirt particles. Then soak the pots for about half an hour in a solution of one part chlorine bleach to three parts water. This will leach out the remaining salts and any harmful soil bacteria. Rinse the pots thoroughly with water and allow them to dry before using them again.

WHEN IT'S TIME TO MOVE . . .

When you're ready to move into a new home, your houseplants will need to be packed as carefully as your china. And if you're moving to another state, you'll need to check with the state's agricultural department for specific requirements pertaining to plants.

Before you move, give your plants a thorough watering; allow excess water to drain off before packing. To prepare small plants for moving, put them into a carton and stuff the area between pots with newspaper to hold them in place. Large plants should be wrapped in sheets of foil or newspaper to help protect the foliage. The potting medium can also be covered to keep it from spilling out of the pot.

Long-distance moves present greater difficulties. Most plants cannot survive a transcontinental trip in a moving van, where they may be subject to darkness and temperature extremes for extended periods. It is safer to transport your plants in a car, so you can make sure they have sufficient water, fresh air and moderate temperatures during the trip.

Some states require a plant certification before they will let plants across their borders, and some states will not admit any plants. Check with the state's department of agriculture before moving.

DISPLAYS IN LIMITED SPACE

Small houses and apartments challenge indoor gardeners who want to grow large numbers of plants. The existing space can be used to create attractive plant displays.

Windowsills that are too small for plant containers can be enlarged—a wide piece of wood attached to the sill will increase shelf space. Or by installing shelf brackets alongside the window, you can create tiers of sunny shelves.

Plants can be suspended from the ceiling in hanging baskets. If you want the plant supports to be invisible, attach the containers to the ceiling with high-strength fishing line.

For areas with low light, simple fluorescent light fixtures can be installed to provide sufficient light for most foliage houseplants. The fixtures can be located in inconspicuous places—beneath cabinets above a kitchen counter, for example.

KEEPING PETS AWAY FROM PLANTS

Cats and dogs are often attracted to houseplant foliage, which can provide pets with a tasty snack. One way to keep animals away is to grow plants such as cacti and succulents that have their own defense system—sharp teeth or spines. But lush, leafy green plants are defenseless, and need some protection. The answer is to prepare a mist solution with a dash of pepper. Add cayenne pepper to water, strain the mix and then spray the plants. Pets dislike the taste of pepper and should avoid the seasoned foliage.

INSECT CONTROL INDOORS

Certain insects and diseases can attack plants even indoors. Insects may enter the home through open windows, and diseases may arise as a result of poor air circulation and wet soil. Although pests and diseases can be controlled with chemicals, it can be hazardous to spray them indoors; chemical sprays may contaminate the air within your house or damage walls, furniture and draperies.

If you have access to an open area outdoors when temperatures are moderate, you can take the plants outside to spray them. But if you must treat your plants in the house, there is a safe and easy way to apply chemicals.

Water the affected plants thoroughly. Then mix the appropriate insecticide or fungicide in a sink, a bucket or other large container. To treat airborne insects or diseases, hold the plant upside down to submerge the foliage in the solution. When the problem is insects or diseases that live in the soil, the entire plant, pot and all, can be submerged. Once the plants are thoroughly wet, they can be removed from the solution and allowed to dry.

EDGE TRIMMING

The leaf tips of houseplants sometimes turn brown, either from a lack of moisture or from excess salts in water and fertilizer. In addition to correcting the problem that caused the leaf tips to turn brown in the first place, you will want to trim off the tips to keep the plant attractive. You can use a pair of scissors to trim away the damaged ends. Instead of making a straight cut across the leaf tip, which will mar the plant's appearance, follow the natural contour of the leaf. From a distance, you will never notice that the foliage has been trimmed.

PREVENTING DRAINAGE DAMAGE

Drainage saucers for potted plants are most commonly made of clay—a material that is cheap and readily available. But clay is a porous material that absorbs water, and this moisture can cause mildew and stains on the surface beneath it. If you use clay saucers under your potted plants, there is a simple way to prevent water damage to your floors and furniture. You can coat the saucers with a sealer, such as shellac, which keeps the clay from absorbing moisture.

TOP DRESSING

When a plant begins to outgrow its pot, it will give you a signal by sending a network of roots through the surface of the soil. If you are not ready to move the plant into a larger container, you can use a temporary measure, called top dressing, to keep the plant healthy. Top dressing is a way to provide fresh soil to the roots at the surface of the container.

To top dress, use a blunt fork to loosen the top 1 to 2 inches of soil in the pot. Remove the loose soil and discard it. Mix fresh soil with a slow-release fertilizer and add this mixture to the pot. Fill the pot to within ¼ inch of the rim. Tamp the soil down lightly and water it well. This top dressing will give the plant a supply of fresh nutrients for approximately two months.

A VACATION FROM HOUSEPLANTS

When the time comes to leave your plants unattended for two or three weeks, a few preparations will help keep them healthy until your return. A plant's foremost requirement is for water, and there are various methods of ensuring an adequate supply.

First, water the plants thoroughly; a long soak in a sink or tub is best. After soaking, one way to conserve moisture is to place the plant in a plastic bag and seal it. If the plant is too large for a plastic bag, enclose the pot and the exposed soil surface in a sheet of plastic. An alternative method of retaining moisture is to place each houseplant, pot and all, in a larger container, and fill the space between the two with thoroughly moistened peat moss or vermiculite. These materials can hold moisture for a lengthy period.

Either of these methods will keep houseplants sufficiently moist for two to three weeks. The plants will also need light, so place the prepared plants in an area that receives some sunlight daily.

5
DICTIONARY OF FOLIAGE HOUSEPLANTS

The tropics and subtropics supply an abundance of beautiful plants that grow indoors, where they are protected from deadly winter cold. In a spot that approximates their native habitat, be it a shadowy, humid jungle floor or a bright desert, these plants will thrive. A key to success is to evaluate the growing conditions you can provide and to choose your plants accordingly. Among the 125 types of plants described and illustrated in the dictionary that follows, you are bound to find many that will grow well in your home as they enliven it with their distinctive colors, forms and textures.

Each entry of the dictionary specifies a plant's light, temperature and humidity requirements. Of the three levels of exposure to natural light referred to in the entries, the most intense is direct light, in which sunlight falls on the plant's foliage for at least four hours a day. The second level of intensity, bright light, is achieved with less than four hours of direct exposure to sunlight each day. In the condition termed limited light, the sun's rays rarely, if ever, fall directly on the plant. For information on how to locate your plants so they get these levels of light, see page 22. Plants needing artificial light should be placed 18 to 24 inches from a fluorescent fixture with two 40-watt tubes that are on for 12 to 16 hours a day. Desirable room temperatures, like natural light, are divided into three levels, with the warm range measuring over 72° F, average ranging from 68° F to 72° F and cool measuring less than 68° F. A relative humidity greater than 50 percent is termed high, a level from 30 to 50 percent is medium, and a low humidity measures less than 30 percent. For information on how to measure and control relative humidity, see pages 20-21.

In addition to light, temperature and humidity, the dictionary specifies the best growing medium for each plant and how often to fertilize, as well as water requirements, repotting and propagation techniques, and any unusual cultural requirements. Entries are arranged alphabetically by the botanical names of the plants, but the dictionary also lists common names, which are cross-referenced to the appropriate entry.

ACORUS GRAMINEUS 'VARIEGATUS'

ADIANTUM CAPILLUS-VENERIS

AECHMEA FASCIATA

AEONIUM ARBOREUM 'ATROPURPUREUM'

Acorus (AK-o-rus)

Moisture-loving, grasslike plant from 6 inches to 2 feet tall. Fan-shaped clumps of flat, sword-shaped foliage, solid green or green with white stripes, emerge from a slender underground stem.

Selected species and varieties. *A. gramineus,* grassy-leaved sweet flag, Japanese sweet flag: has green leaves to 6 inches long. 'Variegatus' has white-striped green leaves to 12 inches long.

Growing conditions. Give Japanese sweet flag bright light, medium humidity and a cool temperature. Keep the soil evenly moist to wet; dried-out soil can cause the leaf tips to turn brown. Check the soil daily for adequate moisture. Fertilize regularly in spring and summer. Propagate by division and use an all-purpose soil mix for potting.

Japanese sweet flag can be damaged by red spider mites, especially if it is grown in a hot, dry environment.

Adiantum (ad-ee-AN-tum)
Maidenhair fern

Dainty fern with lacy green fronds, 6 to 24 inches in length, on glossy black, wiry leafstalks that resemble human hair. Individual leaflets may be fan-shaped, oblong or round.

Selected species and varieties. *A. capillus-veneris,* Venus's-hair: has light green fronds with fan-shaped leaflets ½ inch or less in size. Leaflets are lobed and have delicate teeth along the margins.

Growing conditions. Maidenhair does best in limited light and an average temperature with high humidity. It can be planted in a terrarium, which will keep the humidity high. The soil should be kept evenly moist. Fertilizer may be applied once in spring and once in summer. In late winter, maidenhair can be propagated by division of its crowns and repotted in a fern mix.

Maidenhair is susceptible to aphids, fungus gnats, mealybugs and scale insects. But insecticides can damage maidenhair's delicate foliage; soap spray is a recommended alternative.

Aechmea (EEK-mee-a)

Vase-shaped epiphytic bromeliad to a height of 2 feet. Strap-shaped leaves in a rosette form a cuplike water reservoir. After two years, a flower stalk emerges from the center of the rosette and bears small, inconspicuous pastel flowers between long-lasting bracts.

Selected species and varieties. *A. fasciata,* silver vase: has gray-green leaves with horizontal silver bands. Leaves are covered with a white powdery film. Spiny bracts are pink and remain colorful for months. Powder blue flowers form between the bracts. Flowers turn red as they age and fade quickly. Within two years of flowering, the plant dies.

Growing conditions. Provide silver vase with bright light, medium to high humidity and average room temperature. Keep the potting mix moderately moist during spring and summer and barely moist during winter. Keep the water cup filled with fresh water. Fertilize once a month from spring to fall by adding a diluted water-soluble fertilizer to the water cup. If after two years silver vase has not flowered, place it in a plastic bag with an apple for four to five days in indirect light to encourage budding. Propagate from offsets that form at the base of the plant just before flowering occurs. Repot offsets in a peat-based soilless mix or in sphagnum moss.

Silver vase is susceptible to damage from scale insects.

Aeonium (ee-OH-nee-um)

Green succulent that varies in height from 1 inch to 3 feet, and may form a ground-hugging rosette of fleshy leaves or grow treelike with sparse branches arranged in a loose, open shape. Small, star-shaped flowers are pink, red or yellow and bloom in spring.

Selected species and varieties. *A. arboreum:* grows in a treelike form to 3 feet tall. Branch tips produce rosettes of spoon-shaped, glossy green leaves and bear bright yellow flowers. 'Atropurpureum' has green leaves with tinges of purple.

Growing conditions. Give aeonium direct light, low humidity, a warm temperature in summer and a cool temperature in winter. Let the soil become dry to the touch between thorough waterings. Fertilize once every six weeks in spring and summer. Propagate from seed or stem cuttings and plant in a cactus mix.

Aeonium can be damaged by mealybugs and scale insects. It is susceptible to root and stem rot.

Aeschynanthus
(ess-kuh-NAN-thus)
Basket plant

Vining, trailing or climbing plant with stems from 8 inches to 3 feet in length. Leaves are leathery and grow along the stem in pairs or in whorls.

Selected species and varieties. *A. marmoratus:* trails to 2 feet in length, and has oval green leaves with lighter green veins. Undersides of leaves are flushed with maroon. *A. × hybridus* 'Black Pagoda': grows in a trailing form and has leaves longer than those of *A. marmoratus.*

Growing conditions. Give basket plant bright light, warm room temperature and medium humidity. Keep the potting mix evenly moist but not soggy. Apply fertilizer regularly throughout the year. Propagate by simple layering or from stem cuttings or seed. Pot in a peat-based soilless mix. Repot once every two years.

Basket plant is susceptible to aphids and mealybugs.

—

African milk tree see *Euphorbia*

—

Agave (a-GAH-vee)
Century plant

Erect succulent that forms a stemless rosette of fleshy green leaves that grow from 14 inches to 3 feet long. Leaves often have teeth or threadlike fibers along the edges and sharp spines at the tips. The name century plant is a misnomer; agave takes only 10 years to flower, but rarely blooms when grown indoors.

Selected species and varieties. *A. victoriae-reginae:* grows to 10 inches tall and has dark green leaves with creamy white edges.

Growing conditions. Give century plant direct light, average room temperature and low humidity. Water infrequently but thoroughly and fertilize once a year in spring or summer. Use cactus mix when repotting and wear gloves for protection from the spine-tipped leaves. Propagate from seed or from offsets.

Agave leaves can be damaged by mealybugs and scale insects.

—

Aglaonema (ag-lay-o-NEE-ma)
Chinese evergreen

Compact plant, 1 to 3 feet tall, with multiple leafstalks and oval or lance-shaped, patterned green leaves to 12 inches in length.

Selected species and varieties. *A. commutatum* 'Silver Queen': has dark green leaves with irregular patches of silver. *A. costatum,* spotted Chinese evergreen: forms a dense clump of oval, glossy green leaves flecked with irregular white markings. *A. modestum:* has waxy, dark green leaves.

Growing conditions. Chinese evergreen needs limited light, medium humidity and average temperature. Allow the soil to dry between waterings. Apply fertilizer in spring and summer. Chinese evergreen can be propagated by dividing the plant or by air layering. An all-purpose soil mix should be used for repotting.

Chinese evergreen can be damaged by aphids, mealybugs, scale insects and spider mites. It is susceptible to root rot and stem rot.

—

Alocasia (al-o-KAY-zha)
Elephant's ear

Erect, leafy plant that grows from a thick, fleshy underground stem. Leaves are green with silver, white or brownish black markings. They are shaped like an elephant's ear and grow to 2½ feet wide on slender, pencil-shaped stalks.

Selected species and varieties. *A. cuprea,* giant caladium: grows to 2 feet tall. Leaves are puckered and metallic green with dark purple undersides. Leaf veins are purplish black. *A. sanderana:* grows to 4 feet tall and has metallic black-green leaves 16 inches long and 7 inches wide. Leaves are lobed and have silver edges. Prominent leaf veins are silver-white. Undersides of leaves are purple.

Growing conditions. Provide limited light, a warm temperature and very high humidity. Keep the soil moist. Apply fertilizer in spring and summer. Propagate by division and pot in an all-purpose soil mix.

Elephant's ear can be damaged by mealybugs, scale insects, spider mites and whiteflies.

—

Aloe (AL-o)

Upright green succulent that can grow to several feet in height. Leaves are dagger-shaped, green, 4 to 30 inches long and may have spines.

Selected species and varieties. *A. barbadensis,* also known as *A.*

AESCHYNANTHUS × HYBRIDUS 'BLACK PAGODA'

AGAVE VICTORIAE-REGINAE

AGLAONEMA COMMUTATUM 'SILVER QUEEN'

ALOCASIA CUPREA

ALOE BARBADENSIS

ALTERNANTHERA FICOIDEA 'BETTZICKIANA'

ANANAS COMOSUS
'VARIEGATUS'

ANTHURIUM CRYSTALLINUM

vera, medicine aloe, burn plant: grows to 2 feet tall in stemless clumps. Leaves are fleshy, gray-green, 1 to 2 feet long, 2 to 3 inches wide and have soft teeth along the margins. They contain a jellylike plant tissue that can be used to treat minor skin maladies. *A. variegata,* tiger aloe, partridge breast: a dwarf species that grows to 6 inches tall. Leaves are olive green striped with irregular white bands, grow in clumps and reach 4 inches or more in length.

Growing conditions. Provide aloe with direct light, average room temperature and low humidity. Keep the soil on the dry side; water infrequently. Fertilize in summer. Propagate from offsets. Repot in a cactus mix.

Aloe can be damaged by mealybugs, spider mites and scale insects. It is susceptible to crown rot.

—

Alternanthera
(al-ter-NAN-ther-a)
Joseph's coat, copperleaf

Ground-hugging or erect bushy plant that grows to 12 inches tall. Small, paired leaves are green and variegated with yellow, red, orange, purple or bronze.

Selected species and varieties. *A. ficoidea:* forms a low-growing mat of green leaves that may be highlighted with red, purple or bronze. 'Amoena' grows in a bushy form to 9 inches tall and has reddish brown leaves with red-orange veins and blotches. 'Bettzickiana' grows in a rounded, bushy form. Leaves are narrow, contorted, and may be solid green, cream, pink, salmon-red or a combination of these colors.

Growing conditions. Give Joseph's coat direct light, a warm temperature and average humidity. Keep the soil evenly moist. Fertilize in spring and summer. Pinch the stems back to control leggy growth and encourage bushiness. Propagate from stem cuttings and pot in an all-purpose soil mix.

Joseph's coat is susceptible to aphids, spider mites and whiteflies.

—

Aluminum plant see *Pilea*
Amomum see *Elettaria*

—

Ananas (a-NAN-us)

Erect bromeliad that grows in a rosette to a height of 3 feet and produces pineapples. Leaves are green, stiff, sword-shaped and from 1 to 3 feet in length. A flower spike, bearing pink bracts surrounding blue or pink flowers, emerges from the center of the rosette. Eventually, the spike thickens to form a pineapple, which is topped by a cluster of toothed leaves.

Selected species and varieties. *A. comosus,* pineapple: has dark green leaves with spiny tips. Fruit can grow to 10 inches long. 'Variegatus', variegated pineapple, has ivory-colored margins that turn slightly pink in lavish sunlight.

Growing conditions. Pineapple must have direct light to produce its best leaf color. Provide good air circulation, average humidity and a warm temperature. Allow the surface of the soil to dry slightly between thorough waterings. Fertilize once a month during spring and summer. Propagate from offsets or from a fruit cap sliced from the top of a pineapple *(page 58).* If after three years the plant has not flowered, put it in a plastic bag with an apple and set it in indirect light for four to five days to encourage flowering. Repot in an all-purpose soil mix.

Pineapple is susceptible to damage from scale insects.

—

Angelwings see *Pilea*

—

Anthurium (an-THUR-ee-um)
Tailflower, flamingo flower

Erect, leafy plant to 3 feet in height with pencil-shaped stalks and heart-shaped or tapering leaves up to 18 inches long.

Selected species and varieties. *A. crystallinum,* crystal anthurium, strap flower: has leafstalks to 15 inches long, with heart-shaped, emerald green leaves to 10 inches long. Leaves are prominently marked with a network of thick silver-white veins.

Growing conditions. Strap flower must have limited light, average to warm temperature and high humidity. The potting mix should be kept evenly moist. Mature plants can be fed regularly in spring and summer. Strap flower can be propagated by division and repotted in a peat-based soilless mix.

Strap flower may be attacked by mealybugs, scale insects and spider mites.

Aporocactus (a-por-a-KAK-tus)

Spiny desert cactus with trailing, leafless green stems from 3 to 6 feet long and ½ inch wide. Stems have clusters of brownish bristles on small, slightly raised surface pores. Tubular pink, rose or crimson flowers bloom in spring.

Selected species and varieties. *A. flagelliformis*, rattail cactus: has bright green stems that can grow to 6 feet long. Bristles are ⅛ inch long. Flowers are crimson-pink and 2 to 3 inches in diameter.

Growing conditions. Give rattail cactus direct light; insufficient light will cause spindly, malformed growth. Maintain a warm temperature and low humidity. Allow the soil to dry thoroughly between waterings. Fertilize rattail cactus once a year, in spring. Propagate by taking stem cuttings and pot them in a cactus mix.

Rattail cactus can be damaged by aphids, mealybugs, spider mites, scale insects and thrips. It is susceptible to root and stem rot.

—

Aralia see *Polyscias*

—

Araucaria (ar-a-KAIR-ee-a)

Evergreen tree to 6 feet tall. Branches are covered with needles that may be stiff or soft, and flat or rounded.

Selected species and varieties. *A. heterophylla*, Norfolk Island pine: grows in a symmetrical form with tiers of branches. Needles are bright green, short, soft and rounded.

Growing conditions. Norfolk Island pine does best in bright light and average to cool room temperature with good air circulation. It must have medium humidity; low humidity can cause the needles to turn brown. The soil should be watered thoroughly and allowed to dry to the touch before watering again. Fertilizer should be applied in spring and summer. Frequent turning of the pot will maintain even growth. This tree is slow-growing and needs to be repotted only when it grows too big for its container. Because it is such a slow grower, home propagation is not recommended.

Norfolk Island pine is susceptible to mealybugs, red spider mites and scale insects.

Ardisia (ar-DIZ-ee-a)

A broad genus of about 250 species of tropical broad-leaved evergreen shrubs and trees that can grow to 50 feet in their natural habitat. Only one species can be grown indoors.

Selected species and varieties. *A. crenata*, coralberry: grows to 3 feet tall in a shrubby form and can be pruned into a treelike shape. Leaves are shiny, waxy and from 2 to 4 inches long. Small, star-shaped, fragrant white flowers bloom in summer and are followed by clusters of pea-sized red berries. Berries mature in late December and may remain on the plant until the next crop arrives.

Growing conditions. Coralberry needs bright light in summer and direct light in winter. It does best in cool room temperatures and high humidity. The soil should be kept evenly moist and the plant should be fed regularly in spring and summer; fertilizer will help produce a healthy crop of berries. An all-purpose soil mix can be used for repotting. Coralberry is started from seed by commercial growers under special greenhouse conditions. Home propagation is not recommended.

Coralberry is susceptible to damage from scale insects. It can also get red spider mites if it is grown in a hot, dry environment.

—

Areca palm see *Chrysalidocarpus*
Arrowhead vine see *Syngonium*
Artillery plant see *Pilea*

—

Asparagus (a-SPA-ra-gus)

Feathery-looking green plant that can be erect, climbing or trailing. It resembles a fern, but it is not a fern; it is related to the common edible asparagus. Stems may be branched or unbranched and are covered with delicate, needlelike green foliage. Small white flowers bloom at various times of the year and are followed by brightly colored berries.

Selected species and varieties. *A. densiflorus:* has woody stems to 4 feet long. 'Myers', foxtail asparagus fern, plume asparagus, grows erect in a bushy form with densely covered fronds that grow to 15 inches long. 'Sprengeri', Sprenger asparagus fern, has branched stems, spreading or trailing to 4 feet in length. Berries may be red or orange. *A. myriocladus*, also called *A. macowanii*, feather plume asparagus fern: grows

APOROCACTUS FLAGELLIFORMIS

ARAUCARIA HETEROPHYLLA

ARDISIA CRENATA

ASPARAGUS MYRIOCLADUS

ASPIDISTRA ELATIOR 'VARIEGATA'

ASPLENIUM NIDUS

ASTROPHYTUM ASTERIAS

to 2½ feet with fluffy-looking fronds. *A. setaceous,* also called *A. plumosus,* lace fern: grows upright to 2 feet tall.

Growing conditions. Asparagus fern does best in bright light, average to cool temperature and medium humidity. It can also be grown under fluorescent light. The soil should be kept evenly moist in summer and barely moist in winter; if it is allowed to dry out completely, leaves may turn yellow and drop. Fertilizer can be applied regularly during spring and summer. Asparagus fern can be propagated by division and repotted in an all-purpose soil mix. It is suitable for a hanging basket.

Asparagus fern may be damaged by mealybugs, scale insects and spider mites.

—

Aspidistra (as-pi-DIS-tra)

Stemless, upright plant to about 3 feet tall. Narrow, oblong, glossy green leaves grow on long stalks.

Selected species and varieties. *A. elatior,* cast-iron plant, barroom plant: has dark green leaves that are 2½ feet long and 4 inches across. 'Variegata' has bright green leaves with white stripes.

Growing conditions. Cast-iron plant requires little care and can survive under adverse conditions. It does best in a cool temperature, medium humidity and bright light, but it can adapt to low light. The soil may be kept relatively dry and the plant should be fertilized regularly in spring and summer. Propagate by division and repot in an all-purpose soil mix.

Cast-iron plant is susceptible to mites and scale insects.

—

Asplenium (as-PLEE-nee-um)

Upright green fern that grows to 2 feet tall. Fronds arch outward from a central growing point on black leaf-stalks and may be simple or compound, broad or finely textured.

Selected species and varieties. *A. bulbiferum,* hen-and-chickens fern, mother fern: has sprawling fronds with lacy compound leaves. Plantlets arise from small bulblike structures produced on the upper surface of mature fronds. *A. nidus,* bird's nest fern: has a bowl-shaped rosette of shiny, simple fronds with a brown, hairlike center resembling a bird's nest. Broad, leathery, apple green, wavy-edged fronds are from 1 to 2 feet in length.

Growing conditions. Provide mother fern and bird's nest fern with limited light, an average temperature during the day and a slightly cooler temperature at night. Mother fern requires high humidity and evenly moist soil; dry soil can cause brown spots to develop on the leaves. Bird's nest fern needs medium humidity and can tolerate soil kept slightly drier than for mother fern. Fertilizer should be applied in spring and summer. Repot in a well-drained, prepared fern mix. Propagate by dividing the plant or from plantlets.

Mother fern and bird's nest fern may be damaged by aphids, foliar nematodes, mealybugs and scale insects. They are susceptible to root rot and to excess chlorine and fluoride in tap water.

—

Astrophytum (as-tro-FY-tum)
Star cactus

Squat, rounded, brown or green cactus from 2 to 12 inches tall. The body of the cactus has shallow or deep vertical clefts and may have sharp spines or white hairs. Cup-shaped flowers blossom from the top of the cactus in spring.

Selected species and varieties. *A. asterias,* sand dollar cactus, sea urchin cactus: grows to 2 inches tall and 3 inches wide. Short hairs and dotlike pores cover the gray-green surface. Yellow flowers, sometimes flushed with red, bloom after the cactus is at least three years old. *A. myriostigma,* bishop's cap cactus: grows to 8 inches tall and is divided vertically into five sections, each in the shape of a bishop's cap. White, downy dots cover the silver-green body of the cactus. Flowers are bright yellow.

Growing conditions. Star cactus requires direct light, low humidity, a warm temperature in summer and a cool temperature in winter. Bishop's cap cactus is able to tolerate slightly lower light levels. The soil should be allowed to dry thoroughly between waterings; excessive watering can cause raised, scablike tissue to appear on the cactus. Fertilizer should be applied during the cool-temperature, low-light months of late winter or early spring. The cactus can be propagated by offsets and repotted in a cactus mix.

Star cactus can be damaged by aphids, mealybugs, scale insects, spider mites, bacterial soft rot and scab diseases.

Aucuba (a-KEW-ba)

Small evergreen shrub that grows to 3 feet tall and can be pruned into a treelike shape. Stems and branches bear pairs of oval leaves 3 to 7 inches long and pointed at the ends.

Selected species and varieties. *A. japonica,* Japanese laurel: has glossy dark green, coarsely toothed leaves 7 inches long. 'Variegata', gold dust plant: has glossy green leaves heavily speckled with gold.

Growing conditions. Japanese laurel and gold dust plant tolerate a wide range of temperatures and can survive in an unheated room in an area where winters are mild. They need bright light and low to medium humidity. The soil should be allowed to dry to the touch between thorough waterings. Established plants can be fertilized once every three to four months. They can be propagated from stem cuttings and potted in an all-purpose soil mix.

Japanese laurel and gold dust plant can be damaged by red spider mites, especially if they are kept in a hot, dry location. They are also susceptible to aphids, mealybugs and scale insects.

—

Australian laurel
see *Pittosporum*

Avocado see *Persea*

Baby rubber plant
see *Peperomia*

Baby's tears see *Soleirolia*

Barroom plant see *Aspidistra*

Basket plant see *Aeschynanthus*

Bead plant see *Nertera*

—

Beaucarnea (bo-KAR-nee-a)
Bottle ponytail

Bottle-shaped succulent from 12 inches to 3 feet tall. A tan, woody stem grows from a swollen base that resembles a bulb. Long, narrow, straplike green leaves grow from the top of the stem.

Selected species and varieties. *B. recurvata,* ponytail or elephant-foot tree: has smooth, flat leaves to 6 feet long.

Growing conditions. Provide ponytail with direct light, average room temperature and low humidity. Allow the soil to dry out substantially between thorough waterings; the swollen stem base holds water to protect the plant against drought.

Fertilize once a year in spring or summer. Propagate by offsets and repot in a cactus mix.

Ponytail is susceptible to damage from mealybugs, scale insects, spider mites and whiteflies.

—

Begonia (be-GO-nee-a)

A broad genus of green plants that range from 4 inches in height to several feet tall. The leaves range in size from 1 to 10 inches long and may be rounded, triangular or irregular, and can be dull, shiny, smooth or quilted. Airy sprays or clusters of small white, pink, red and even greenish flowers bloom from summer to early spring. Some species flower year round.

Two types of begonias are grown indoors: fibrous-rooted and rhizomatous begonias. Fibrous-rooted begonias have a network of thin roots. Rhizomatous begonias have rhizomes, which are thick, fleshy, modified stems that produce roots. The rhizomes may grow wholly or partially underground.

Selected species and varieties. *B. boweri,* eyelash begonia: grows in a bushy form to approximately 6 inches tall. Leaves are irregular in shape and size and velvety dark green with blotches of a lighter green color. Leaf margins have soft, arching ¼-inch-long hairs that resemble eyelashes. Clusters of tiny pink flowers blossom in late winter and early spring. Roots are rhizomatous. *B. coccinea,* angel-wing begonia: grows upright to 3 or 4 feet. Long green stems have knotted joints similar to those on bamboo stems. Leaves are ear-shaped, leathery and green, with silvery white spots on the upper surfaces and purplish red spots on the undersides. Drooping clusters of long-lasting, waxy, coral red flowers are produced on red flower stalks in summer. Roots are fibrous.
B. × erythrophylla, beefsteak begonia: grows to 12 inches in height. Leaves are smooth, fleshy, shaped like lily pads and covered with fine red hairs. Upper surfaces are glossy green with veins in a pattern like the fingers of a hand. Undersides are red. Small light pink flowers are produced in late winter and early spring. Roots are rhizomatous. *B. masoniana,* iron-cross begonia: grows in a bushy mound from 6 to 12 inches tall. Leaves are puckered, covered with fine hairs and have a brown pattern resembling a cross in the center. White flowers may bloom indoors.

AUCUBA JAPONICA 'VARIEGATA'

BEAUCARNEA RECURVATA

BEGONIA × REX-CULTORUM

BRASSAIA ACTINOPHYLLA

BUXUS MICROPHYLLA JAPONICA

CALADIUM × HORTULANUM

Roots are rhizomatous. *B. × rex-cultorum,* rex begonia: grows 12 to 15 inches tall. Leaves may be blotched, spotted or marbled in various colors including green, silver, gray, bronze, reddish brown or purple. Flowers are pink or white. Roots are rhizomatous.

Growing conditions. Most begonias need bright light, medium humidity, average temperatures by day and slightly cooler temperatures at night. Rex begonias need limited light, a warm temperature and high humidity. The soil should be watered thoroughly and allowed to dry to the touch between waterings. Begonias should be fertilized regularly during spring and summer. Fibrous-rooted begonias can be propagated by division or from stem cuttings. Rhizomatous begonias can be propagated by division of the rhizome, or from leaf cuttings and leaf-vein cuttings *(page 44).* An all-purpose soil mix can be used for repotting.

Begonias can be damaged by mealybugs, scale insects, whiteflies, edema and powdery mildew disease. They are also susceptible to fungal and bacterial diseases if they are subject to a combination of wet soil and high humidity.

■

Belgian evergreen see *Dracaena*

Bird-catcher tree see *Pisonia*

Bird's nest fern see *Asplenium*

Bishop's cap cactus see *Astrophytum*

Bloodleaf see *Iresine*

Blushing bromeliad see *Neoregelia*

Boston fern see *Nephrolepis*

Botanical wonder see *Fatshedera*

Boxwood see *Buxus*

■

Brassaia (BRASS-ee-a)

Tropical shrub that grows from 6 to 10 feet tall and can be trained into a treelike shape. Narrow, long leafstalks produce shiny green compound leaves from 6 to 12 inches long. Each compound leaf is made up of five to seven leaflets.

Selected species and varieties. *B. actinophylla,* also known as *Schefflera actinophylla,* schefflera, Australian umbrella tree, queen's umbrella tree, Queensland umbrella tree: grows to 8 feet in height and has

leaflets that radiate from a central point like the spokes on an umbrella.

Growing conditions. Schefflera does best in bright light and can adapt to lower light, but too little light can result in legginess. The plant needs a warm temperature and high humidity. The soil should be watered thoroughly, then allowed to dry substantially before the next watering. Fertilizer can be applied year round. Schefflera can be propagated from seed or by air layering and repotted in an all-purpose soil mix.

Schefflera is very susceptible to spider mites, especially if it is kept in a hot, dry room. It can also be damaged by mealybugs, scale insects and whiteflies. Schefflera can get bacterial, fungal and viral infections, and crown and stem rot.

■

Buddhist pine see *Podocarpus*

Burn plant see *Aloe*

Burro's tail see *Sedum*

Button fern see *Pellaea*

■

Buxus (BUK-sus)
Boxwood

Small evergreen tree or compact shrub that grows 3 inches to 6 feet tall, with oval, glossy green leaves about 1 inch long.

Selected species and varieties. *B. microphylla japonica,* Japanese boxwood: grows from 3 inches to 3 feet tall and is well suited for dish gardens.

Growing conditions. Give boxwoods direct light year round, average room temperature and medium to high humidity. Allow the soil to dry moderately between thorough waterings. Fertilize once a month throughout the year. Prune frequently to maintain the desired plant shape. Propagate from stem cuttings and use an all-purpose soil mix.

Boxwoods are susceptible to mealybugs and scale insects.

■

Caladium (ka-LAY-dee-um)

Erect, leafy plant to 2 feet tall. Thick underground tubers produce long stalks with heart-shaped to arrow-shaped, paper-thin leaves.

Selected species and varieties. *C. × hortulanum,* fancy-leaved caladium: has leaves to 15 inches in length in shades of white, green, red and combinations of colors. The margins of the leaves may be ruffled, wavy or flat.

Growing conditions. Caladium needs bright light, high humidity, a warm temperature during the day and a cool night temperature of approximately 65° F. The soil should be evenly moist, but not soggy. Fertilizer can be applied throughout spring and summer. Rotating the plant daily helps maintain even growth and good form. During the winter months, when the foliage dies back, caladium should be stored in a cool, dark, dry room. It can be propagated by division of the tubers in spring and planted in an all-purpose soil mix.

Caladium is generally free from pests and diseases.

Calathea (kal-a-THEE-a)

Upright, leafy green plant to 2 feet tall. Slender leafstalks form clumps in the center of the pot. Leaves have variegated markings that can take the form of bands, streaks, patches, spots or stripes.

Selected species and varieties. *C. makoyana,* peacock plant: has broad, oval leaves from 6 to 10 inches long. Leaves are light green with a dark green band along the edges. Each leaf has dark green oval patches in a pattern that vaguely resembles the markings on a peacock's feather. Dark green lines run from the center of each leaf to the leaf edge in a V shape. Undersides of the leaves are marked with maroon. *C. roseopicta:* grows to 8 inches tall and has short leafstalks that bear dark green leaves. Leaves have red margins and red midribs that change to silvery pink as leaves mature. Undersides of leaves are purple. *C. picturata:* has leafstalks 3 to 4 inches tall. Leaves are 6 inches long, deep olive green and have silvery lines along the midrib and the margins.

Growing conditions. Calathea does best in bright light; exposure to direct sunlight for long periods can bleach the leaves. It needs average to warm room temperature and high humidity. The soil should be medium moist, neither dry nor soggy. Fertilizer can be applied regularly during spring and summer. Calathea can be propagated by division, and an all-purpose soil mix may be used for repotting.

Calathea is relatively insect- and disease-free.

Callisia (ka-LISS-ee-a)
Inch plant

Trailing plant to 3 feet long. Succulent stems support solid green or variegated, pointed oval leaves that are 1 to 8 inches long. Young leaves grow erect, but droop as they mature.

Selected species and varieties. *C. elegans,* also sold as *Setcreasea striata,* striped inch plant: has 2-foot-long stems with olive green leaves to 1½ inches long. Upper leaf surfaces are striped lengthwise with white lines, and the undersides are purple. The foliage is covered with soft, velvety hair.

Growing conditions. Provide inch plant with average to warm room temperature, medium humidity, direct light in winter and bright light the rest of the year. Keep the soil evenly moist but not soggy. Fertilize in spring and summer. Propagate by taking stem cuttings or by dividing the plant. Use an all-purpose soil mix for repotting. Inch plant is suitable for a hanging basket.

Inch plant is susceptible to damage from mealybugs, scale insects, spider mites and whiteflies.

Cardamom see *Elettaria*

Carica (KAIR-i-ka)
Papaya

Tropical tree to 5 feet tall. The erect, polelike trunk bears a crown of broad, lobed green leaves on long stems. Each leaf may have up to seven lobes. Fruit is rarely produced on trees grown indoors.

Selected species and varieties. *C. papaya:* has leaves up to 20 inches across.

Growing conditions. Papaya needs direct light, a warm temperature and medium to high humidity. The soil should be kept moderately to evenly moist, and the plant should be fertilized in spring and summer. Papaya benefits from being placed outdoors in summer, which can help produce lush foliage. Papaya can be propagated from seed saved from store-bought fruit. The seeds should be planted in an all-purpose soil mix to which sand has been added.

Papaya is susceptible to aphids, mealybugs, scale insects and thrips.

Caricature plant
see *Graptophyllum*

CALATHEA MAKOYANA

CALLISIA ELEGANS

CARICA PAPAYA

CARYOTA MITIS

CEPHALOCEREUS SENILIS

CEROPEGIA WOODII

CHAMAEDOREA ELEGANS

Caryota (KAIR-ee-O-ta)
Fishtail palm

Asiatic palm that grows to 12 feet tall and produces clusters of slender, arching green stems. Leaves occur at intervals along the stems; they are up to 2 feet wide and have jagged ends that resemble fishtails.

Selected species and varieties. *C. mitis,* Burmese fishtail palm: has gray-green stems to 7 feet tall and light green leaves.

Growing conditions. Give fishtail palm bright light and medium to high humidity. Keep the temperature warm and the soil evenly moist but not soggy. Fertilize regularly from spring to fall. Propagate from offsets. Repot in an all-purpose soil mix.

Fishtail palm is subject to attack by mealybugs, mites and scale insects.

Cast-iron plant see *Aspidistra*
Century plant see *Agave*

Cephalocereus
(sef-a-lo-SEER-ee-us)

Hairy cactus to 18 inches tall with a round to columnar leafless stem divided lengthwise into numerous grooved sections. Each stem section is covered with long white or yellow hairs that conceal sharp spines.

Selected species and varieties. *C. senilis,* old man cactus: has a stem that grows up to 12 inches tall and is divided into 12 or 15 sections. The woolly stem hairs are 3 to 4 inches in length. They are white and turn brown with age. The concealed spines are 1 to 1½ inches long.

Growing conditions. Old man cactus requires direct light and a warm temperature. It needs little humidity and little water; the soil should be allowed to dry between waterings. The cactus may be fed just once a year in spring. It can be propagated by offsets or from seeds and repotted in a cactus mix.

Old man cactus is susceptible to mealybugs, scale insects and soft rot.

Ceropegia (seer-o-PEE-gee-a)

Vining succulent with threadlike, climbing or trailing stems to 6 feet long. Stems grow from a woody, wrinkled gray base 2 inches across. Leaves are green, small and fleshy, rounded or heart-shaped, and appear at 3-inch intervals along the stem.

Selected species and varieties. *C. sandersonii,* parachute plant: climbs from 4 to 6 feet in height and has mottled green leaves. Flowers are green, resemble tiny parachutes and bloom in summer. *C. woodii,* rosary vine, string-of-hearts: has trailing stems to 3 feet long. Stems develop round, fleshy structures that resemble rosary beads. Upper surfaces of the leaves are marbled with silver; undersides are purple.

Growing conditions. Give parachute plant and rosary vine bright to direct light; insufficient light will result in off-color leaves or elongated stems with few leaves. Provide medium humidity, an average day temperature and a slightly cooler temperature at night. Water thoroughly, then let soil dry to the touch before watering again. Fertilize once a month in spring and summer. Propagate from stem cuttings. Repot in a cactus mix.

Parachute plant and rosary vine are vulnerable to attack by mealybugs and mites.

Chamaedorea
(kam-a-DOR-ee-a)

Slender feathery palm with canelike stems to 3 feet tall. Graceful arching green fronds grow to 18 inches long.

Selected species and varieties. *C. elegans,* parlor palm: has broad, sprawling fronds. 'Bella' grows in a more erect, compact form to a height of 2 feet.

Growing conditions. Parlor palm needs bright light; it can tolerate lower light, but may become spindly over a period of time. It does best in a warm temperature, high humidity and evenly moist soil. The leaf tips can turn brown as a result of insufficient water and low humidity. Parlor palm should be fertilized regularly in spring and summer. It can be propagated by division of the multiple stems or from offsets and repotted in an all-purpose soil mix.

Parlor palm is susceptible to spider mites, especially if the air is dry. It can also attract mealybugs, scale insects and thrips, and can develop Gliocladium rot.

Chamaerops (KAM-a-rops)

Stiff, spiny-stemmed palm with multiple stems that emerge from a fiber-covered base. At the top of each stem is a dark green, fan-shaped frond. Each frond is divided into many sword-shaped sections. Only one species is grown as a houseplant.

Selected species and varieties. *C. humilis,* European fan palm: grows to 4 feet in height with fronds 15 inches long and 2 feet wide.

Growing conditions. European fan palm does best in direct light, but it can adapt to lower light once it becomes accustomed to growing indoors. It needs a warm temperature, and medium to high humidity. The soil should be kept evenly moist but not soggy. Fertilizer should be applied during spring and summer. When the plant becomes potbound, it can be propagated by division of the multiple stems and repotted in an all-purpose soil mix.

European fan palm is vulnerable to attack by mealybugs, mites, scale insects and thrips.

Chandelier plant see *Kalanchoe*

China doll see *Radermachera*

Chinese evergreen
see *Aglaonema*

Chinese fan palm see *Livistona*

Chinese fountain palm
see *Livistona*

Chlorophytum (klor-o-FY-tum)

Trailing green plant 12 to 15 inches high. Thick, fleshy roots produce narrow, strap-shaped leaves from 6 to 18 inches in length. Leaves can be green, white, yellow or striped. In spring and summer, trailing yellow stems to 2 feet long emerge between the leaves and produce star-shaped white flowers at the ends.

Selected species and varieties. *C. comosum,* spider plant: has bright green leaves. Spider plant gets its name from its plantlets, which resemble spiders. 'Vittatum' has 6- to 12-inch, medium green leaves, each with a wide white or cream-colored stripe down the center.

Growing conditions. Give spider plant bright light throughout the year. Provide average humidity and average room temperature. Allow the soil to dry to the touch between thorough waterings. Apply fertilizer once each season. Propagate by simple layering or by separating the plantlets that succeed the flowers. Use an all-purpose soil mix for repotting. Spider

plant is suitable for a hanging basket.

Spider plant is susceptible to damage from scale insects.

Cholla see *Opuntia*

Chrysalidocarpus
(kri-sal-i-doh-KAR-pus)

Graceful feathery palm with clumps of slender, reedlike canes that bear arching, shiny, strap-shaped green fronds. Only one species is grown as a houseplant.

Selected species and varieties. *C. lutescens,* areca palm, yellow palm: grows to 6 feet tall with light green fronds to 4 feet in length.

Growing conditions. Give areca palm bright light, warm room temperature and medium humidity. Keep the soil evenly moist but not soggy; wet, cold soil can cause the leaves to turn yellow. Fertilize regularly during spring and summer. Propagate from offsets. Areca palm grows slowly, about 6 inches a year, and needs repotting only when it outgrows its pot. It can become potbound without adverse effects. Use an all-purpose soil mix for repotting.

Areca palm is subject to damage by aphids, whiteflies and salt buildup.

Cissus (SISS-us)
Grape ivy

Climbing, trailing or vining green plant to 8 feet long. Smooth, velvety or leathery leaves from 2 to 6 inches in length grow from woody stems. Leaves may be solid green or variegated. Most species have curly tendrils that can anchor the plant to any convenient support.

Selected species and varieties. *C. antarctica,* kangaroo vine: grows in a trailing form. Leaves are leathery, slightly toothed, 3 to 4 inches long and have pale green undersides. *C. discolor,* trailing begonia vine: is a slender climber with dark red stems and tendrils. Leaves are velvety, pointed ovals 4 to 7 inches long and green with silver markings on the upper surfaces and pinkish purple on the undersides. Despite its common name, trailing begonia bears no relation to the genus *Begonia. C. rhombifolia,* grape ivy: has glossy dark green leaves with rust-colored hairs on the undersides. Tendrils have forked tips. 'Ellen Danica' has 5-

CHAMAEROPS HUMILIS

CHLOROPHYTUM COMOSUM 'VITTATUM'

CHRYSALIDOCARPUS LUTESCENS

CISSUS RHOMBIFOLIA

CITRUS MITIS

CODIAEUM VARIEGATUM PICTUM

COFFEA ARABICA

inch-long leaves that are deeply lobed and resemble those of an oak tree.

Growing conditions. Most grape ivies do best in bright light but they can adapt to limited light. They need average room temperature, average humidity and soil kept on the dry side. Trailing begonia vine needs direct light, a warm temperature, high humidity and evenly moist soil. Grape ivies should be fertilized once in spring and once in summer. The stem tips can be pinched back regularly to keep the plants bushy. They can be propagated from stem cuttings and repotted in an all-purpose soil mix. Grape ivies are suitable for growing in hanging baskets.

Grape ivies are vulnerable to damage by mealybugs and spider mites and they also are susceptible to salt buildup.

—

Citrus (SIT-rus)

Broad-leaved evergreen tree that grows to 6 feet tall and produces grapefruit, lemons, limes or oranges. Leafstalks may be flattened and flaring or rounded. Leaves are pointed ovals 3 to 6 inches long and aromatic when bruised. Fragrant white flowers appear in late spring and are followed in summer by yellow, orange or green fruit. Flowers and fruit may or may not be produced indoors; if they are, the fruit is usually not full-sized.

Selected species and varieties. *C. mitis,* Calamondin orange: grows to 3 feet tall and produces miniature oranges. *C. × paradisi,* grapefruit: grows to 5 feet. Flattened leafstalks 1 inch long support glossy green leaves 4 inches long. Fruit is yellow, light orange or greenish and has a smooth rind. *C. sinensis,* orange: grows to 5 feet and has flattened 1-inch leafstalks with shiny green 4-inch leaves. Stems have sharp spines. Fruit ranges from pale to deep orange, and the rind may be smooth or rough.

Growing conditions. Give citrus direct light, average temperature and medium to high humidity. The foliage benefits from a move outdoors in summer into bright light, but not searing sun. Keep the soil moderately moist. Fertilize regularly in spring and summer. Propagate from seeds saved from store-bought fruit and plant them in an all-purpose soil mix.

Citrus is susceptible to spider mites, especially if it is grown in dry air; it can also get mealybugs and scale insects. Citrus is vulnerable to scab disease.

Codiaeum (ko-dee-EE-um)
Croton

Bushy, tropical shrub that grows to 3 feet high. A single erect stem supports short-stalked, glossy, leathery leaves from 3 to 18 inches long. Leaves are generally narrow and may be linear or twisted, lobed or unlobed, and smooth or crinkled. They are variegated in various patterns with yellow, green, red, pink, orange, brown, cream or a combination of these colors.

Selected species and varieties. *C. variegatum pictum:* has shiny green leaves with prominent red or yellow ribs and pink, orange, red or yellow variegation.

Growing conditions. To develop its best leaf coloring, croton needs direct light, a warm temperature and medium to high humidity. It thrives in medium-moist soil, but it can tolerate a wide variation in the soil moisture level. Feed regularly from early spring to late summer. Propagate by taking stem cuttings or by air layering. Repot in standard mix.

Croton is vulnerable to attack by mealybugs, scale insects and spider mites.

—

Coffea (KOF-ee-a)
Coffee

Tropical shrub or tree that grows to a height of 15 feet in its natural habitat and bears coffee beans. Woody stems bear glossy green, pointed leaves that are 3 to 6 inches long and 2 inches wide. Fragrant, white star-shaped flowers bloom in summer. Coffee beans are rarely produced on plants grown indoors.

Selected species and varieties. *C. arabica,* common coffee plant: grows in a bushy form to 4 feet in height. Leaves are dark green.

Growing conditions. Give coffee plant direct light year round, high humidity and an average to warm temperature. Keep the soil evenly moist but not soggy. Fertilize regularly from spring through fall. Propagate from seeds or stem cuttings. Start seeds or cuttings in an all-purpose soil mix.

Coffee plant is suceptible to damage from mealybugs, scale insects and spider mites.

—

Coffee see *Coffea*

Coleus (KO-lee-us)

Shrubby tropical plant to 3 feet tall. Fleshy stems bear leaves that may be narrow, oval or rounded, with serrated or smooth edges, and range from 1 to 4 inches long. Small blue flower spikes may bloom in summer.

Selected species and varieties. *C. × hybridus,* garden coleus: has soft, thin, pointed to oval leaves that may be green, pink, cream, yellow, orange, brown, red or a combination of these colors.

Growing conditions. Coleus requires bright light; it can also be grown in fluorescent light. It needs average room temperature and high humidity. The soil should be kept evenly moist but not soggy. Fertilizer should be applied regularly in spring and summer. The flower buds and stem tips can be pinched off to promote fullness. Coleus can be propagated from stem cuttings or from seed and potted in an all-purpose soil mix.

Coleus can get mealybugs, spider mites and whiteflies. It is also susceptible to root and stem rot.

—

Copperleaf see *Alternanthera*
Coralberry see *Ardisia*

—

Cordyline (kor-di-LY-nee)

Shrub or treelike plant that usually has a single erect stem. Leaves are graceful, arching, lance-shaped, and from 1 to 3 feet long and up to 4 inches wide. They may be green, red, copper, cream, pink, bronze or a combination of these colors.

Selected species and varieties. *C. terminalis,* ti plant, good luck plant: grows 2 to 6 feet tall and has green leaves variegated in shades of red, pink, cream or copper.

Growing conditions. To maintain its best leaf coloring, ti plant needs direct light, average to warm room temperature and high humidity. The soil should be allowed to dry slightly between thorough waterings. Fertilizer should be applied in spring and summer. Ti plant can be propagated from ti logs—short sections of the stem, available at garden centers—or by air layering. An all-purpose soil mix can be used for repotting.

Ti plant is susceptible to damage from aphids, mealybugs, scale insects and spider mites.

Corn plant see *Dracaena*

—

Crassula (KRASS-yew-la)

Sprawling, bushy or treelike succulent to 3 feet in height. Fleshy stems support green, blue-gray or yellow leaves that can be spoon-shaped, sickle-shaped, rounded, triangular or linear.

Selected species and varieties. *C. argentea,* jade plant: grows in a treelike form with woody branches and rubbery, shiny jade green leaves, sometimes edged in red. Leaves are oblong and 1 to 2 inches long. 'Tricolor' has green leaves tinged with pink. *C. lycopodioides,* rattail: grows to 9 inches in height and has cylindrical, slender, branching stems covered with tiny, pointed leaves. 'Variegata' has green leaves with vertical cream bands.

Growing conditions. Jade plant and rattail do best in direct light; they can also be grown in fluorescent light. They need average room temperature and low humidity. Allow the soil to dry between waterings; excess water can cause soft, weak stem growth and root rot. Fertilizer should be applied regularly through spring and summer. Jade plant can be propagated from leaf cuttings *(page 41);* both jade plant and rattail can be propagated from stem cuttings and repotted in a cactus mix.

Jade plant and rattail are subject to attack from aphids, mealybugs, scale insects and spider mites.

—

Creeping Charlie see *Pilea*
Cretan brake fern see *Pteris*
Croton see *Codiaeum*
Crown of thorns see *Euphorbia*

—

Cryptanthus (krip-TAN-thus)
Earth-star

Low-growing terrestrial bromeliad with flattened, star-shaped rosettes of stiff, jagged-edged leaves from 3 to 20 inches long.

Selected species and varieties. *C. bivittatus:* has wavy, greenish brown or cream-striped leaves with a pink tint. The leaves grow to 4 inches long. *C. × 'It',* color-band cryptanthus: has green leaves with cream and pink stripes.

Growing conditions. Earth-star adapts to various light conditions, but

COLEUS × HYBRIDUS

CORDYLINE TERMINALIS

CRASSULA ARGENTEA 'TRICOLOR'

CRYPTANTHUS BIVITTATUS

CYANOTIS KEWENSIS

CYCAS REVOLUTA

CYPERUS ALTERNIFOLIUS

CYRTOMIUM FALCATUM

bright light enhances its leaf color. It requires average room temperature and high humidity. The potting mix should be allowed to dry substantially between thorough waterings, and the plant should be fertilized in spring and summer. Earth-star can be propagated from offsets and repotted in a peat-based soilless mix or in sphagnum moss.

Earth-star is vulnerable to damage by scale insects.

—

Curly palm see *Howea*

—

Cyanotis (sy-a-NO-tis)

Low-growing, compact creeping plant to 9 inches in length. Leaves may be oval or triangular and grow to 2 inches long. Stems and leaves are covered with downy hairs.

Selected species and varieties. *C. kewensis,* teddy bear plant: grows in a trailing form and has gray-green leaves with purple undersides. Leaf hairs are reddish brown.

Growing conditions. Teddy bear plant requires direct light, average temperature and very high humidity. It should not be misted; direct application of moisture can damage the hairy leaves. The soil should be allowed to dry moderately between waterings. Fertilizer should be applied once or twice in spring or summer. Teddy bear plant can be propagated by stem cuttings that include at least three pairs of leaves. The cuttings should be planted in an all-purpose soil mix. Established plants rarely need repotting.

Teddy bear plant can be damaged by aphids and mealybugs.

—

Cycas (SY-kus)

Palmlike plant that grows to 3 feet in height. Arching compound fronds to 3 feet in length emerge from a stubby trunk that looks like a pineapple. Leaves are feather-shaped and stiff but springy.

Selected species and varieties. *C. revoluta,* Sago palm: has glossy dark green leaves. Individual leaflets are needlelike, from 3 to 6 inches long and arranged in a V shape along a prominent vein in the center of the leaf.

Growing conditions. Give Sago palm bright light all year long. Provide an average room temperature and low to medium humidity. Water thor-

oughly, then allow the soil to dry moderately before watering again. Fertilize Sago palm once a month from early spring to late summer. Repot once every other year in a combination of half cactus mix and half all-purpose soil mix. Handle the plant carefully; the foliage bruises easily. Sago palms are propagated commercially from seed. They are such slow growers that home propagation is not recommended.

Sago palm can be attacked by mealybugs or scale insects. It is also susceptible to salt buildup.

—

Cyperus (sy-PEER-us)

Semiaquatic, grasslike plant from 10 inches to 4 feet in height. Stems are long, green and topped with leaflike bracts that resemble the spokes on an umbrella.

Selected species and varieties. *C. alternifolius,* umbrella plant: grows 2 to 4 feet tall and has narrow, light green leaflike bracts about 4 inches long.

Growing conditions. Umbrella plant does best in bright to direct light all year long, with an average temperature and high humidity. This is one plant that is nearly impossible to overwater; the soil should be kept moist, and the plant is suitable for growing in a water garden or an aquarium. Fertilizer should be applied once a month in spring and summer. The stems can be cut back to the roots if the plant begins to look shabby; new foliage will grow from the roots. Umbrella plant is propagated by division and can be repotted in an all-purpose soil mix.

Umbrella plant is susceptible to damage from mealybugs, scale insects, spider mites and whiteflies.

—

Cyrtomium (sir-TOH-mee-um)

Leathery-leaved fern that grows erect to a height of 3 feet. Furry leafstalks support 2-foot-long fronds. Leaves are green, 4 inches long and grow in pairs.

Selected species and varieties. *C. falcatum,* holly fern: has glossy, dark green, jagged-edged leaves that resemble holly leaves.

Growing conditions. Holly fern can tolerate low light, dry air and drafts, but it does best in bright light, average to cool temperature and medium humidity. The soil should be allowed to dry moderately between thorough waterings. Holly fern should be fed only occasionally throughout the year. It can be propagated by division and repotted in a fern mix.

Holly fern is susceptible to aphids, mealybugs and scale insects.

—

Dallas fern see *Nephrolepis*

Date palm see *Phoenix*

—

Davallia (da-VAL-ee-a)

Feathery green fern from 9 to 20 inches tall. Furry brown stems, ½ to ¾ inch thick, grow horizontally along the soil surface. The stems, called rhizomes, resemble the feet of a rabbit or a squirrel. Lacy compound fronds grow from 9 to 12 inches long.

Selected species and varieties. *D. fejeensis,* rabbit's-foot fern: has medium green triangular fronds and trailing rhizomes. *D. trichomanoides,* squirrel's-foot fern: has dark green fronds. Rhizomes are covered with white to tannish brown fur.

Growing conditions. Provide rabbit's-foot and squirrel's-foot fern with limited light or grow them under fluorescent lights. Give them average room temperature and medium humidity. Keep the soil barely moist and fertilize occasionally throughout the year. Propagate by cutting sections from the rhizomes. Use a fern mix for potting. Rabbit's-foot fern is suitable for hanging baskets.

Rabbit's-foot and squirrel's-foot fern can get aphids, mealybugs and scale insects. They are susceptible to damage from salt buildup.

—

Desert fan palm
see *Washingtonia*

Devil's backbone
see *Pedilanthus*

Devil's ivy see *Epipremnum*

—

Dieffenbachia
(deef-en-BOK-ee-a)
Dumbcane

Leafy green plant that grows to 6 feet tall. When young it has a single stout stem; when mature it may have multiple stems. Leaves are variegated and grow to 1½ feet long.

Selected species and varieties. *D. amoena,* giant dumbcane: has dark

green, oblong leaves with an irregular creamy white pattern that radiates from the center of the leaves. *D.* × *bausei:* grows to 3 feet tall, with lance-shaped green leaves that have yellow-green markings. Leaf edges are dark green with irregular dark green splotches and random white speckles. *D. exotica,* exotic dumbcane: grows in a compact form to 2 feet tall. Leaves are dark green and nearly covered with white or greenish white variegation. *D. maculata,* spotted dumbcane: grows to a height of 4 feet and has dark green leaves with white markings. 'Rudolph Roehrs', yellow-leaf dumbcane, has bleached-looking chartreuse leaves dappled with ivory and bisected by a dark green center line. Leaf edges are dark green.

Growing conditions. Dumbcane can adapt to various growing conditions, but it does best in bright but diffused light, average temperature and medium to high humidity. The soil can be allowed to approach dryness between thorough waterings, but it should not dry out completely. Fertilizer should be applied in spring and in summer. Dumbcane can be propagated from stem cuttings and by air layering. An all-purpose soil mix can be used for potting.

Dumbcane exudes a poisonous sap and should not be grown in a household that has small children.

Dumbcane is susceptible to mealybugs and spider mites. It is also subject to bacterial stem blight and stem rot, leaf spot and salt buildup.

—

Dionaea (dy-o-NEE-a)
Venus flytrap

One-species genus of carnivorous bog plant that grows to 4 inches tall. Each leaf has a crease down the center spine and several teeth along the edges. When an insect alights on a leaf, the leaf snaps shut. The plant digests the insect through leaf glands, then resets its trap. Each trap has a limited life; after closing three or four times, the trap turns black and dies, but the plant continually produces new traps.

Selected species and varieties. *D. muscipula:* has light green leaves tinged with red along the inside folds. White flowers are produced in late spring.

Growing conditions. Venus flytrap needs bright light, cool temperature, high humidity and a constantly moist growing medium; it does best in a terrarium. The planting medium

DAVALLIA FEJEENSIS

DIEFFENBACHIA EXOTICA

DIONAEA MUSCIPULA

DIZYGOTHECA ELEGANTISSIMA

DRACAENA MARGINATA 'TRICOLOR'

DROSERA ROTUNDIFOLIA

should be sphagnum moss. If Venus flytrap does not catch insects, it should be fertilized once a week during spring and summer with a balanced, water-soluble fertilizer. It can be propagated by division of its underground bulbs.

Venus flytrap is not susceptible to damage by insects, since it consumes them; but it can develop powdery mildew.

—

Dizygotheca
(diz-ee-go-THEE-ka)
False aralia

Lacy-looking, treelike plant to 6 feet tall and 20 inches wide. Slender, unbranched stems have long stalks with narrow leaflets arranged in a circle at the tips of the leafstalks.

Selected species and varieties. *D. elegantissima:* has jagged leaflets ½ inch wide that are coppery red when young and a dark green when mature.

Growing conditions. False aralia needs bright light, warm room temperature and high humidity. The soil should be allowed to dry to the touch between thorough waterings. Fertilizer can be applied once a month in spring and summer. False aralia does not adapt well to being moved or repotted, so it should be repotted only once every few years. An all-purpose soil mix can be used for repotting. False aralia is propagated commercially from seed under special growing conditions, and home propagation is not recommended.

False aralia is susceptible to mealybugs, scale insects, spider mites and thrips.

—

Dracaena (dra-SEE-na)

Shrubby or treelike plant from 20 inches to 10 feet tall. Most species have single unbranched stems that may be either succulent or woody. Narrow, arching leaves grow to 2 feet long. They may be solid green or green with stripes or spots.

Selected species and varieties. *D. deremensis:* grows to 6 feet tall with shiny green, strap-shaped leaves to 18 inches long. 'Janet Craig' has slightly broader, darker green leaves. 'Warneckii', striped dracaena, has gray-green leaves about 1 foot long with two narrow white stripes. *D. fragrans massangeana,* corn plant: grows to 5 feet tall on a thick, woody stem. Leaves

are bright green with a broad yellow stripe and are about 2 feet long and 4 inches wide. *D. marginata,* red-margined dracaena, dragon tree: grows to 9 feet tall on a straight or curving woody stem. Leaves are sword-shaped, 2 feet long and ½ inch wide, and green with red margins. 'Tricolor' has pink-, cream- and green-striped leaves. *D. sanderana,* Belgian evergreen, ribbon plant: grows to 3 feet tall. Slender, upright stems support narrow, lance-shaped leaves that grow to 9 inches long and are green bordered with white stripes. *D. surculosa,* also called *D. godseffiana,* gold dust plant: looks very different from other dracaenas. It does not grow more than 20 inches tall. Wiry stems support oval, spotted green leaves that are 3 inches long and 1½ inches wide.

Growing conditions. All dracaenas thrive in bright light; 'Janet Craig' and 'Warneckii' can gradually adapt to limited light. All need an average to warm temperature and medium to high humidity for new leaf growth, which is inhibited in cool, dry air. The soil should be kept moderately dry and fertilizer should be applied once every three months in spring and summer. Dracaenas can be propagated by air layering and from stem cuttings and offsets. An all-purpose soil mix can be used for repotting.

Most dracaenas are subject to damage from mealybugs, scale insects and spider mites. They are also susceptible to leaf spot disease and salt buildup.

—

Dragon tree see *Dracaena*

—

Drosera (DRAH-ser-a)
Sundew

Carnivorous bog plant from 2 to 12 inches tall. Leaves and stems are tipped with sticky, green to reddish hairs that can trap and digest insects.

Selected species and varieties. *D. binata:* has long, thin stems that split into a T shape at the ends. Stems may be maroon or green. *D. filiformis:* has green stems that are curled at the ends. *D. rotundifolia,* round-leaved sundew: has ground-hugging rosettes of bronze leaves ½ to 2 inches long. Leaves have rounded ends, are ½ inch wide and resemble tentacles. Hairs are red.

Growing conditions. Sundew needs bright light, an average temperature and high humidity. The soil mix should be kept moist to wet at all times to simulate sundew's natural environment; a bottle garden or terrarium is an ideal location. The planting medium should be sphagnum moss. If sundew does not catch insects, it should be given fertilizer once a week in spring and summer. It can be propagated from seed, from leaf cuttings or by division.

Sundew is sensitive to aerosol sprays; do not use pesticides on it. It is rarely damaged by pests, but it can get powdery mildew.

—

Dumbcane see *Dieffenbachia*

Earth-star see *Cryptanthus*

Elephant-foot tree
see *Beaucarnea*

Elephant's ear see *Alocasia*

—

Elettaria (el-e-TAIR-ee-a)

Erect, leafy shrublike herb to 3 feet tall. Stems are canelike and grow in dense clumps. Leaves are long, narrow and green.

Selected species and varieties. *E. cardamomum,* also known as *Amomum cardamomum,* cardamom: has bright green leaves that grow to 15 inches long and 3 inches wide.

Growing conditions. Cardamom thrives in bright light and can adapt to limited light. It needs a cool temperature and medium humidity. The soil should be allowed to dry to the touch between thorough waterings. Fertilizer should be applied monthly in spring and summer. Cardamom can be propagated from seed or by division. An all-purpose soil mix may be used for repotting.

Cardamom is susceptible to mealybugs and spider mites.

—

English ivy see *Hedera*

—

Epipremnum (ep-i-PREM-num)
Pothos, devil's ivy

Leafy green plant with multiple stems that grow to 6 feet in length and may be climbing or trailing. Leaves are oval to heart-shaped, 3 to 8 inches long, olive green or medium green with yellow, cream or white markings, and may be glossy or matte.

Selected species and varieties. *E. aureum,* formerly *Scindapsus au-*

reus, golden pothos: has glossy green leaves with irregular yellow markings. 'Marble Queen' has shiny bright green leaves with white swirls and streaks.

Growing conditions. Pothos needs bright light, medium humidity and average room temperature. It can also be grown under fluorescent light. The soil can be kept on the dry side. Pothos needs to be fertilized only two or three times during spring and summer. It can be propagated by simple layering and from stem cuttings and planted in an all-purpose soil mix. It is suitable for a hanging basket and will attach itself to a slab of tree bark or other support.

Pothos is generally free from pests and diseases.

—

Euonymus (yew-ON-i-mus)
Spindle tree

Broad-leaved evergreen shrub from 18 inches to 4 feet tall. Stiff woody stems produce several branches that bear small oval green leaves with yellow or white variegation.

Selected species and varieties. *E. japonica,* Japanese spindle tree: has leathery leaves to 2 inches long and 1 inch wide. Leaves have slightly jagged edges and are bordered in white. 'Mediopicta' has dark green leaves with a bright yellow patch in the center of each leaf.

Growing conditions. Provide spindle tree with bright light, cool room temperature and medium humidity. Allow the soil to become slightly dry between waterings; too much water can cause the leaves to drop. Fertilize monthly during spring and summer. Prune spindle tree liberally to maintain its compact shape, and repot once every other year in an all-purpose soil mix. Propagate from stem cuttings.

Spindle tree is vulnerable to mealybugs and spider mites, especially if it is grown in a warm environment with low humidity. It can also get powdery mildew.

—

Euphorbia (yew-FOR-bee-a)

Large genus that includes 1,600 species of smooth and spiny shrubs and cactuslike succulents from 4 inches to 6 feet tall.

Selected species and varieties. *E. lactea,* hatrack euphorbia: grows in a treelike form to 6 feet tall and resembles a hatrack. A greenish white,

ELETTARIA CARDAMOMUM

EPIPREMNUM AUREUM

EUONYMUS JAPONICA 'MEDIOPICTA'

EUPHORBIA MILLII

× FATSHEDERA LIZEI 'VARIEGATA'

FATSIA JAPONICA

FAUCARIA TIGRINA

wavy stripe runs down the center of the stem, which is spiny and scalloped. Minute leaves, less than ½ inch in length, grow between the spines. *E. millii,* crown of thorns: grows in a shrubby form to 36 inches tall on a thick stem. The stem and the branches are covered with sharp spines. Narrow green leaves to 2½ inches long emerge from the stem and branch tips; the leaves drop as the plant matures. Tiny red or yellow flowers bloom in summer. *E. tirucalli,* pencil tree: grows to 5 feet tall and has a single green stem that branches into smooth, pencil-thick green tips. Tiny leaves emerge and drop randomly; the plant is bare most of the time. *E. trigona,* African milk tree: is shaped like a candelabra. Spiny triangular stem has pale green to white wavy stripes that fade with age. Spoon-shaped, ¼-inch leaves are produced along the stem.

Growing conditions. Hatrack euphorbia, crown of thorns and pencil tree need direct light, average room temperature and low humidity. Keep the soil fairly dry between waterings. Fertilize in spring and summer. Repot only when the plant outgrows its pot and use a cactus mix. Propagate from stem cuttings.

Hatrack euphorbia, crown of thorns and pencil plant have a milky white sap that can irritate the skin. To keep it from bleeding out of the plant while propagating, apply cold water or powdered horticultural charcoal to the wound on the parent plant. The cuttings may also be dipped in cold water or powdered charcoal. The cuttings should then be allowed to dry for 24 hours before planting.

Hatrack euphorbia, crown of thorns and pencil tree are all relatively insect- and disease-free.

———

European fan palm
see *Chamaerops*

False aralia see *Dizygotheca*

Fan palm see *Chamaerops; Livistona; Washingtonia*

———

× Fatshedera (fats-HED-e-ra)
Botanical wonder

A single-species genus that is a genetic cross of *Fatsia japonica* and *Hedera helix.* It is a large-leaved, rangy plant to 4 feet tall with woody stems that bear long-stalked leaves. The leaves are glossy green, 8 inches wide and have up to five lobes.

Selected species and varieties. × *F. lizei:* grows in a shrubby form but with climbing stems. 'Variegata' has green leaves with irregular white patches in the center.

Growing conditions. Give botanical wonder bright to direct light or grow it under fluorescent light. Maintain an average room temperature and medium humidity. Let the soil dry slightly between thorough waterings; leaves may drop if the soil is too wet or too dry. Fertilize regularly in spring and summer. Stake botanical wonder plant if the stem needs support and pinch the leaves back to maintain a bushier appearance. Propagate from woody stem cuttings and repot in an all-purpose soil mix.

Botanical wonder may be attacked by aphids, mealybugs, scale insects and spider mites.

———

Fatsia (FAT-see-a)

Green-leaved shrub to 5 feet tall. A single, woody stem supports long leafstalks and huge leaves from 8 to 18 inches wide. Each leaf is lobed, with up to nine deep clefts.

Selected species and varieties. *F. japonica,* Japanese fatsia: has glossy dark green leaves.

Growing conditions. Fatsia needs bright to direct light; it can also be grown under fluorescent light. It does best in cool to average room temperature with low to medium humidity. The soil can be kept moderately dry. Fertilizer should be applied regularly during spring and summer. Fatsia can be propagated from seed and from stem cuttings and repotted in an all-purpose soil mix. Care should be taken when handling fatsia. Its new leaves are tender and bruise easily; bruising can permanently mar the appearance of the foliage.

Fatsia is vulnerable to attack by aphids, mealybugs, scale insects and spider mites.

———

Faucaria (faw-KAIR-ee-a)

Low-growing succulent 3 inches tall that forms a star-shaped rosette. Leaves are fleshy, triangular, green and 1 to 2 inches long. Yellow daisy-like flowers bloom in spring.

Selected species and varieties. *F. tigrina,* tiger's jaw: has sharp teeth along the margins of the leaves, which are gray-green, speckled with white and resemble open jaws. *F. tuberculosa:* has gray-green leaves covered with yellowish white dots and several teeth along the margins.

Growing conditions. Give tiger's jaw direct light year round. Provide a warm temperature and low humidity. Allow the soil to dry between thorough waterings. Apply fertilizer no more than once a month; too much fertilizer causes soft, weak growth. Repot every two to three years in a cactus mix. Propagate by division.

Tiger's jaw can be damaged by mealybugs or scale insects and is susceptible to leaf rot.

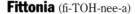

Ficus (FY-kus)

Genus that includes milky-sapped trees, shrubs and vines that may be erect to 15 feet tall with woody stems or ground-hugging to 1 inch tall with thin, stringy stems. Leaves are green and may be oval, rounded, heart-shaped or fiddle-shaped, and from 1 inch to 15 inches long.

Selected species and varieties. *F. benjamina,* weeping fig: grows to 15 feet tall and can be trained as a tree or a shrub. Graceful, arching branches support smooth, glossy, apple green leaves that are 2 to 4 inches long and slightly wavy, oval and pointed at the ends. 'Variegata' has green leaves with irregular cream-colored patches. *F. deltoidea,* mistletoe fig: grows to 3 feet tall and has dark green, rounded leaves 1 to 3 inches long. Yellow-gray fruit the size of a pea can appear year round. *F. elastica,* rubber plant: has a single stem that grows erect to 6 feet tall. Leaves are glossy, dark green and leathery, from 6 to 10 inches long. 'Decora', bread-leaf rubber plant, grows to 6 feet in height and has 15-inch leaves that emerge from a red protective sheath. When the leaves first open, they are bronze; as they mature, they turn dark green on the upper surface and red underneath. They have a prominent ivory-colored vein down the center. 'Variegata' has drooping green leaves with a yellow border and patches of yellow. *F. lyrata,* fiddle-leaf fig: has a single stem that grows erect to 8 feet tall. Leaves are glossy green, about 15 inches long, 9 inches wide and shaped like violins. *F. pumila,* creeping fig: is a trailing or climbing vine that has papery, heart-shaped leaves to 1 inch long. *F. retusa nitida,* Indian laurel: grows in a shrubby form to 4 feet tall. Leaves are shiny, rounded and about 3 inches in size.

Growing conditions. Most figs, rubber plants and Indian laurel need direct light, medium humidity and average to warm temperature. The soil can be allowed to dry between waterings, and fertilizer should be applied three times a year: once in spring, once in summer and once in fall. Creeping fig can take lower light than other figs, even shade, as long as the soil is kept evenly moist. It can also tolerate a temperature as low as 35° F. It requires more fertilizer than other figs and should be fed regularly during spring and summer.

Rubber plants and fiddle-leaf and mistletoe figs can be propagated by air layering. Creeping fig, weeping fig and Indian laurel can be propagated from stem cuttings. An all-purpose soil mix can be used for repotting. Figs often drop leaves when they are moved or transplanted and should be repotted only when their roots appear through the surface of the soil or when they become top-heavy.

All figs, rubber plants and Indian laurel can get mealybugs, scale insects, spider mites and thrips. They are susceptible to edema and salt buildup.

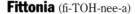

Fig see *Ficus*
Fishhook pincushion cactus
see *Mammillaria*
Fishtail palm see *Caryota*

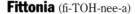

Fittonia (fi-TOH-nee-a)

Mounded or creeping plant to 6 inches. Succulent stems bear egg-shaped leaves up to 3 inches long. Green leaves have a network of prominent veins in shades of red, white or silver.

Selected species and varieties. *F. verschaffeltii,* red-nerve plant: has olive green leaves with pinkish red veins. *F. verschaffeltii argyroneura,* mosaic plant, silver-nerve plant: has dark green leaves with delicate white or silver veins. 'Minima' has leaves less than 1 inch long.

Growing conditions. Give nerve plant limited to bright light or grow it under fluorescent light. Provide medium to high humidity and a warm temperature; it is suitable for a terrarium, which will keep the humidity high. Keep the potting mix moderately moist; allow it to dry only slightly between waterings. Fertilize nerve plant regularly throughout the year. Propagate from stem cuttings and pot in a peat-based soilless mix.

Nerve plant is susceptible to dam-

FICUS BENJAMINA 'VARIEGATA'

FITTONIA VERSCHAFFELTII ARGYRONEURA

GIBASIS PELLUCIDA

GRAPTOPHYLLUM PICTUM

GREVILLEA ROBUSTA

GYNURA AURANTIACA

age from mealybugs and mites. It can also get crown rot.

—

Flamingo flower see *Anthurium*
Freckle-face see *Hypoestes*
Geranium see *Pelargonium*
German ivy see *Senecio*

—

Gibasis (ji-BAY-sis)

Leafy, fine-textured trailing plant that grows to 2½ feet long. Slender stems bear delicate green leaves. Dainty white flowers, ¼ inch in size, are produced in profusion.

Selected species and varieties. *G. pellucida* (formerly *G. geniculata* and *Tripogandra multiflora*), Tahitian bridal veil: has oval ½-inch leaves with purple undersides.

Growing conditions. Tahitian bridal veil does best in bright to direct light; it can also be grown under fluorescent light. It needs an average temperature and medium humidity. The soil should be allowed to dry to the touch between thorough waterings. Fertilizer should be applied regularly throughout the year. Dried leaves can be removed from the plant as they accumulate. The stem tips can be pinched back to encourage bushiness. Tahitian bridal veil can be propagated by division and repotted in an all-purpose soil mix.

Tahitian bridal veil can get mealybugs, scale insects, spider mites and whiteflies.

—

Gold dust plant see *Aucuba; Dracaena*
Good luck plant see *Cordyline; Sansevieria*
Grapefruit see *Citrus*
Grape ivy see *Cissus*

—

Graptophyllum
(grap-toh-FIL-um)

Erect evergreen shrub that grows to several feet tall in its native habitat. Only one species is grown as a houseplant.

Selected species and varieties. *G. pictum,* caricature plant: grows to 30 inches tall. Leaves are glossy green and variegated with yellow. They are oval, pointed at the ends and grow to 6 inches long.

Growing conditions. Provide caricature plant with bright light, high humidity, a warm temperature and an evenly moist potting medium. Fertilize once a month during spring and summer. Propagate from stem cuttings and repot in a peat-based soilless mix.

Caricature plant is vulnerable to mealybugs and spider mites.

—

Grevillea (gre-VIL-ee-a)
Spider flower

A genus of about 250 evergreen shrubs and timber trees that can reach 150 feet in their natural environment. Only one species is grown as a houseplant.

Selected species and varieties. *G. robusta,* silk oak tree: grows to its full height of 6 feet in three or four years. Lacy, fernlike foliage is silky to the touch. Leaves resemble fronds and are from 5 to 14 inches long.

Growing conditions. Silk oak tree needs bright to direct light, a cool temperature, good air circulation and medium to high humidity. The soil should be allowed to dry slightly between thorough waterings. Fertilizer can be applied regularly during spring and summer. Silk oak tree should be transplanted every spring to a pot at least 2 inches bigger than its previous pot to allow for the plant's vigorous growth. An all-purpose soil mix can be used for repotting. Silk oak tree is started from seed in greenhouse conditions by commercial growers; home propagation is difficult and not recommended.

Silk oak tree can be attacked by mealybugs or spider mites.

—

Gynura (ji-NEW-ra)

Trailing plant to 6 feet in length. Branching stems support velvety green leaves that are covered on both sides with purple hairs. Pungent, orange-yellow flowers are produced in late spring or early summer.

Selected species and varieties. *G. aurantiaca,* purple velvet plant, purple passion vine: grows erect when young and gradually becomes trailing to 3 feet in length as it matures. Leaves are 4 to 8 inches long, 4 inches wide and have jagged edges.

Growing conditions. To maintain its coloration, purple velvet plant needs bright light. It needs high humidity and a warm temperature; the foliage can be damaged if the temperature drops below 55° F. The soil should be kept evenly moist. Care should be exercised when watering; splashes of water may leave permanent marks on the leaves. A fertilizer should be applied once a month during spring and summer. Purple velvet plant can be propagated from stem cuttings. An all-purpose soil mix can be used for repotting.

Purple velvet plant is susceptible to aphids, mealybugs, scale insects, spider mites, whiteflies and leaf spot.

—

Hare's-foot fern see *Polypodium*

—

Haworthia (ha-WOR-thee-a)
Wart plant

Low-growing plant from 3 to 7 inches tall that forms a rosette of narrow, triangular green leaves to 4 inches long. Leaves may be soft and fleshy or hard and rough, warted or non-warted and spiny or spineless.

Selected species and varieties. *H. angustifolia:* has leaves to 2 inches long with vertical white lines. *H. fasciata,* zebra haworthia: grows to 4 inches tall. Leaves are dark green with raised white horizontal lines from tip to base.

Growing conditions. Give wart plant bright to direct light or grow it under fluorescent light. Maintain a warm daytime temperature, a cooler temperature at night and low humidity. Allow the soil to dry between thorough waterings. Fertilize once a year in spring or summer. Propagate from offsets and pot in a cactus mix.

Wart plant can get mealybugs, scale insects and spider mites. It is susceptible to salt buildup.

—

Hedera (HED-er-a)
Ivy

Evergreen vine that may be climbing or trailing. Stems are woody, between 4 and 10 feet in length and produce aerial roots that will attach to any slightly moist surface. Leaves are generally leathery and arrow-shaped, often have three lobes, and may be green or variegated.

Selected species and varieties. *H. canariensis,* Algerian ivy: has glossy green leaves that grow to 5 inches long and 6 inches across. Stems are burgundy. 'Gloire de Marengo', also known as 'Variegata', has gray-green leaves with creamy white markings. *H. helix,* English ivy:

has leaves that range from ¾ inch to 4 inches long and have three, five or seven lobes. Stems generally produce many short branches, which give the vine a bushy appearance. 'Buttercup' has bright yellow to yellow-green leaves with three or five lobes. 'Glacier' has gray-green leaves with white margins and three lobes. 'Gold Dust' has leaves that are green mottled with yellow and have three lobes. 'Harald' has light green leaves with cream-colored margins and three lobes. 'Needlepoint' has small leaves that grow to 1 inch long and have three sharply pointed lobes. 'Parsley Crested' has apple green leaves with curled edges and five lobes. 'Pixie' grows to only 10 inches in length and has leaves that are ¾ inch long and may have three, five or seven lobes. 'Scutifolia', sweetheart ivy, has dark green leaves that are heart-shaped and have no lobes.

Growing conditions. Ivies need bright light, and the variegated types need direct light to maintain their best leaf color. Ivies can tolerate a wide range of temperatures, but they do best in slightly cool room temperature. They need medium humidity. If the air is dry, the leaf tips may turn brown. The soil should be kept evenly moist. Fertilizer should be applied regularly during spring and summer. Ivies can be grown in hanging baskets or trained to climb on supports. They can be propagated from stem cuttings and by simple layering. An all-purpose soil mix may be used for potting.

Ivies may be damaged by mealybugs, scale insects and spider mites. They are susceptible to edema and salt buildup.

—

Heimerliodendron see *Pisonia*

—

Hemigraphis (hem-i-GRAF-is)

Fleshy, red-stemmed plant that grows prostrate to 1 foot long. Leaves are heart-shaped with jagged edges and grow in pairs on 1-inch leafstalks.

Selected species and varieties. *H.* 'Exotica', purple waffle plant: has green puckered leaves that are tinged with purple on the upper surfaces and burgundy on the undersides. Leaves grow to 3 inches in length and 2 inches in width.

Growing conditions. Purple waffle plant thrives in bright light; it can also

HAWORTHIA FASCIATA

HEDERA HELIX

HEMIGRAPHIS 'EXOTICA'

117

HOWEA FORSTERANA

HOYA CARNOSA 'VARIEGATA'

HYPOESTES PHYLLOSTACHYA

be grown under fluorescent light. The stems can become spindly if the light level is too low. High humidity and an average to warm temperature year round are needed. The potting mix can be allowed to dry slightly between thorough waterings. Fertilizer should be applied monthly during spring and summer. Purple waffle plant can be propagated from stem cuttings and repotted in a peat-based soilless mix.

Purple waffle plant can get spider mites, especially if it is grown in a warm, dry location.

Hen-and-chickens fern
see *Asplenium*

Heptapleurum see *Schefflera*

Hindu rope plant see *Hoya*

Holly fern see *Cyrtomium*

Howea (HOW-ee-a)
Sentry palm

Dark green, feather-leaved palm to 8 feet tall and 6 feet wide. It has deeply cleft, arching fronds that grow from a single stem.

Selected species and varieties. *H. belmoreana,* Belmore sentry palm, curly palm: has a short-stemmed trunk with a thick base. leafstalks are erect, 10 to 18 inches long and bear graceful, erect, bright green fronds to 18 inches in length. *H. forsterana,* Kentia palm: has fronds that reach 2 feet in length and spread horizontally from the stem.

Growing conditions. Give sentry palm limited to bright light, an average temperature and medium humidity. Allow the soil to dry between thorough waterings and fertilize during spring and summer. Shower the palm regularly to keep the fronds clean. Repot once every two to three years and use an all-purpose soil mix. Sentry palm is a slow grower and not recommended for home propagation; commercially, it is started from seed under special greenhouse conditions.

Sentry palm is vulnerable to attack from mealybugs, scale insects and spider mites.

Hoya (HOY-a)
Wax vine

Twining, trailing vine to 6 feet in length. Leathery green leaves to 3 inches long appear in pairs along flexi-ble, woody stems. Clusters of fragrant, star-shaped flowers are produced just above a pair of leaves, usually in summer. Vines usually reach 3 feet before flowering.

Selected species and varieties. *H. carnosa,* wax plant: grows to 5 feet long. Leaves are glossy, dark green, slightly wavy, oval and pointed at the ends. Flowers are pinkish white and have red centers. 'Variegata', variegated wax plant, has leaves that may be solid green, creamy yellow or a combination of the two. 'Krinkle Kurl', Hindu rope plant, has leaves that are twisted and curled.

Growing conditions. Wax plant and Hindu rope plant must have direct light, average room temperature and low humidity. The soil should be kept moderately dry; soggy soil can cause root rot. Fertilizer should be applied occasionally during spring and summer; excess fertilizer can cause the flower buds to drop from the plant. Wax plant and Hindu rope plant can be propagated by simple layering or from stem cuttings. An all-purpose soil mix may be used for repotting. Both of these vining plants are suitable for a hanging basket.

Wax plant and Hindu rope plant can get aphids, mealybugs, scale insects and spider mites. They are susceptible to root rot.

Hypoestes (hy-po-ES-teez)

Erect, shrubby plant to 3 feet tall. Leaves are oval, 2 inches long, speckled and grow in pairs on short leafstalks.

Selected species and varieties. *H. phyllostachya,* polka-dot plant, freckle-face: has dark green leaves covered with pink dots.

Growing conditions. Polka-dot plant requires bright light to maintain its best leaf coloration. It needs average room temperature and medium humidity. The soil should be allowed to dry slightly between waterings; if the soil becomes too dry, the leaves may wither. Fertilizer should be applied regularly during spring and summer. Polka-dot plant gets leggy with age; it looks best if it is kept pruned to a height of about 2 feet. It can be propagated from seed and from stem cuttings. An all-purpose soil mix can be used for repotting.

Polka-dot plant is susceptible to mealybugs, scale insects, spider mites and whiteflies.

Inch plant see *Callisia*

Indian laurel see *Ficus*

—

Iresine (ir-e-SY-nee)
Bloodleaf

Upright, shrubby plant to 2 feet tall. Stems are succulent and red. Leaves are rounded and dark red or greenish red with red or yellow veins.

Selected species and varieties. *I. herbstii*, beefsteak plant: has 2-inch leaves that are dark red with pale red veins. The leaves may be puckered and have wavy edges. 'Aureoreticulata', chicken gizzard, has red leaves tinged with green and yellow veins.

Growing conditions. Provide beefsteak plant and chicken gizzard with direct sun; if the light level is too low, the plants will get spindly and weak. Maintain an average temperature and medium humidity. Allow the soil to become dry to the touch between thorough waterings and fertilize regularly during spring and summer. Pinch back the growing tips regularly for a full, bushy appearance. Propagate from stem cuttings and repot in an all-purpose soil mix.

Beefsteak plant and chicken gizzard are susceptible to aphids, mealybugs and scale insects.

—

Ivy see *Hedera*

Jade plant see *Crassula*

Japanese laurel see *Aucuba*

Joseph's coat see *Alternanthera*

—

Kalanchoe (kal-an-KO-ee)

Shrubby succulent from 12 inches to 3 feet in height, in low-growing rosettes or on erect stems. Leaves are fleshy and may be oval, rounded or triangular, and green, gray-green or red.

Selected species and varieties. *K. daigremontiana*, mother of thousands: grows to 3 feet tall on erect stems. Leaves are oval, light green and bear tiny plantlets all along the margins. *K. tomentosa*, panda plant: forms ground-hugging rosettes of thick, stubby leaves covered with soft silver hairs. When the plant is young, the leaf margins are tipped with rusty orange hairs; as it matures, the hairs turn chocolate brown. *K. tubiflora*, chandelier plant: grows to 36 inches tall on an erect stem. Leaves are tubular and green

covered with red spots. Tiny plantlets grow at the leaf tips.

Growing conditions. Kalanchoe needs direct sun, average room temperature and low humidity. The soil can be allowed to dry substantially between waterings. Fertilizer should be applied regularly in spring and summer. Kalanchoe can be propagated from stem cuttings, plantlets and leaf cuttings *(page 41)*. A cactus mix should be used for repotting.

Kalanchoe can be damaged by aphids, mealybugs, scale insects and spider mites. It is susceptible to powdery mildew.

—

Kangaroo vine see *Cissus*

Kentia palm see *Howea*

Lace fern see *Asparagus*

Lady palm see *Rhapis*

—

Leea (LEE-a)

Genus of over 70 species of evergreen shrubs or small trees to several feet in height. Only one species is grown as a houseplant.

Selected species and varieties. *L. coccinea*, West Indian holly: grows in a shrubby form to 6 feet tall. Woody stems bear dark green leathery leaves to 4 inches long. Leaves are oval, pointed at the ends and have wavy edges. Flower buds are deep red and open into rose red or pink flower clusters. 'Rubra' has metallic green leaves with maroon undersides. Stems are maroon.

Growing conditions. West Indian holly needs bright light, average room temperature and high humidity. The soil should be kept slightly moist but not soggy. Fertilizer can be applied once a month in spring and summer. Commercial growers start West Indian holly from seed in special greenhouse conditions; home propagation is not recommended.

West Indian holly can be damaged by mealybugs and spider mites.

—

Lithops (LITH-ops)
Stone plant, living stones

Stubby, rounded succulent that grows only 2 inches tall and resembles small desert rocks. Two very thick, fleshy leaves grow from an underground stem and are fused at the base. Leaves are gray, beige or brownish yellow. Daisylike flowers

IRESINE HERBSTII

KALANCHOE TOMENTOSA

LEEA COCCINEA 'RUBRA'

LITHOPS TURBINIFORMIS

LIVISTONA CHINENSIS

MAMMILLARIA ELONGATA

MANGIFERA INDICA

emerge from the slit between the two leaves in late summer. After a flower dies, the leaves surrounding it die. New leaves promptly replace the old ones, and new flowers emerge the following summer.

Selected species and varieties. *L. turbiniformis:* grows to 1 inch tall. Leaves are tan with dark brown markings on their flat-topped surface. Flowers are bright yellow.

Growing conditions. Provide stone plant with direct light, an average temperature and low humidity. Water infrequently and let the soil dry out between waterings; overwatering causes roots and stems to rot. Propagate from seed or by separating offsets. Pot in a cactus mix.

Stone plant is slow-growing, and needs repotting only once every three or four years. It does not require any fertilizer.

Stone plant can be damaged by mealybugs and scale insects.

—

Living stones see *Lithops*

—

Livistona (liv-i-STO-na)
Fan palm

Tropical palm tree that can grow to 60 feet or more in its native habitat. Fronds are fan-shaped and deeply cleft into long, narrow leaf segments that droop at the tips.

Selected species and varieties. *L. chinensis,* Chinese fan palm, Chinese fountain palm: grows to 6 feet tall. Leafstalks are 15 inches in length and have sharp spines along the edges. Fronds are glossy green, 2 feet long and 2 feet wide.

Growing conditions. Chinese fan palm thrives in bright light, average room temperature and medium humidity. The soil can be allowed to dry between waterings. Fertilizer should be applied regularly during spring and summer. Repotting can be done once every two to three years and an all-purpose soil mix may be used. Home propagation is not recommended; Chinese fan palm is a very slow grower and is best started from seed under greenhouse conditions.

Chinese fan palm is susceptible to mealybugs, nematodes, scale insects and spider mites.

—

Maidenhair fern see *Adiantum*

Mammillaria (mam-i-LAIR-ee-a)

Globular or cylindrical cactus that grows to 10 inches tall and from 2 inches to several feet wide. Short spines cover the surface. Small flowers bloom in spring and form a circle around the top of the cactus.

Selected species and varieties. *M. bocasana,* powder puff cactus, snowball cactus: grows in a globular form to 2 inches in diameter. Spines are silky and white. Flowers are yellow, bell-shaped and ¾ inch long. *M. elongata,* golden star: has cylindrical stems to 4 inches high covered with radial yellow spines ½ inch long. Flowers are yellow. *M. wildii,* fishhook pincushion cactus: grows in a cylindrical form to 6 inches in height and 2½ inches in diameter. Spines are yellowish. Flowers are white.

Growing conditions. Provide powder puff and fishhook pincushion cactus with direct light, an average to warm temperature and low humidity. Water infrequently and allow the soil to dry between waterings. Apply fertilizer once a year in spring. Propagate from seed or from offsets. Repot infrequently, about once every three years, when the plant outgrows its pot, and use a cactus mix.

Powder puff and fishhook pincushion cactus can be damaged by mealybugs and scale insects. They are also susceptible to root rot.

—

Mangifera (man-JIF-er-a)

Tropical evergreen tree with an erect, woody trunk and leathery green leaves that may be oval or narrow and lance-shaped. Flowers and fruit are rarely produced indoors.

Selected species and varieties. *M. indica,* mango: grows to a height of 5 feet. Leaves are glossy dark green, lance-shaped and 12 inches in length.

Growing conditions. Give mango bright light, an average temperature and medium to high humidity. Water thoroughly, then allow the soil to dry moderately before watering again. Fertilize regularly during spring and summer. Propagate from the seed of a fresh store-bought mango. Use an all-purpose soil mix for planting.

Mango is vulnerable to aphids, mealybugs, scale insects and thrips.

—

Mango see *Mangifera*

Maranta (ma-RAN-ta)

A leafy, low-growing green plant to 12 inches tall. Short leafstalks, sheathed at the base, support broad, oval leaves that are 5 inches long and 3 inches wide. Leaves are green with gray or red veins and symmetrical featherlike markings.

Selected species and varieties. *M. leuconeura,* prayer plant: grows to 12 inches in height. Upper leaf surfaces are marked with yellow-green, dark green or brown patches. Undersides may be gray or purple. Leaves fold in the evening in a form that resembles hands in a praying position. *M. leuconeura erythroneura,* red-veined prayer plant: has light green leaves with bright red veins and yellow markings along the center of the leaf. Undersides are reddish purple. *M. leuconeura kerchoviana,* rabbit's foot, rabbit's tracks, prayer plant: has light green leaves with brown markings resembling a paw print. Undersides of leaves are gray-green.

Growing conditions. Prayer plants do best in bright light, average room temperature and medium to high humidity. The soil should be kept evenly moist but not soggy; wet soil can cause root rot. Fertilizer should be applied regularly in spring and summer. Prayer plants can be propagated by division. An all-purpose soil mix can be used for repotting. Prayer plants are suitable for terrariums.

Prayer plants are subject to attack by aphids, mealybugs, scale insects and spider mites. They are also susceptible to salt buildup and root rot.

—

Marble plant see *Neoregelia*
Medusa's head see *Tillandsia*

—

Mimosa (mi-MO-sa)

Genus of about 500 herbs, shrubs, trees and vines. Only one species is grown as a houseplant.

Selected species and varieties. *M. pudica,* sensitive plant: grows erect and shrublike to 20 inches tall. Prickly stems support long-stalked, light green, ferny-looking foliage. Foliage recoils on contact; the leaves fold inward and the leafstalks droop temporarily.

Growing conditions. Sensitive plant requires bright to direct light, warm room temperature and medium to high humidity. The soil should be kept moderately moist and allowed to dry only slightly between waterings.

Fertilizer can be applied regularly in spring and summer. Sensitive plant can be propagated from seed or from stem cuttings. It should be repotted when the roots protrude through the drainage hole.

Sensitive plant can be damaged by mealybugs and scale insects.

—

Monstera (mon-STAIR-a)

Trailing or climbing vine to 6 feet tall. Aerial roots form on mature plants; some will attach to any nearby support. Long leafstalks bear glossy green leaves that are heart-shaped or rounded.

Selected species and varieties. *M. deliciosa,* split-leaf philodendron (in spite of its common name, it is not a member of the genus *Philodendron),* Swiss cheese plant: has 12-inch leafstalks and broad leaves that may be as much as 18 inches in width. Leaves are heart-shaped. As they grow older, the leaves develop deep clefts and perforations. These perforations are the plant's way of coping with high winds in nature, because the perforations allow air to pass through the leaves without tearing them. *M. obliqua:* has elongated leaves that range up to 8 inches in length and 3 inches in width. The leaves develop perforations with age.

Growing conditions. Give split-leaf philodendron bright light in summer and direct sun in winter, or grow it under fluorescent light. Maintain a warm room temperature and medium to high humidity. Water thoroughly and allow the soil to dry before watering again. Fertilize plants regularly from spring until fall. Propagate from stem cuttings or by air layering or simple layering. Pot in an all-purpose soil mix. Provide a tree bark or moss-covered support for the aerial roots to cling to.

Split-leaf philodendron can be attacked by aphids, mealybugs, scale insects, spider mites and thrips.

—

Mosaic plant see *Fittonia*
Moses-in-the-cradle see *Rhoeo*
Mother fern see *Asplenium*
Mother-in-law's tongue
see *Sansevieria*
Mother of thousands
see *Kalanchoe*

MARANTA LEUCONEURA ERYTHRONEURA

MIMOSA PUDICA

MONSTERA DELICIOSA

NEOREGELIA CAROLINAE 'TRICOLOR'

NEPHROLEPIS EXALTATA

NERTERA GRANADENSIS

OPUNTIA MICRODASYS
'ALBISPINA'

Neoregelia (nee-o-re-JEE-lee-a)

Epiphytic bromeliad 9 to 12 inches in height and 2½ feet wide. Leaves are sword-shaped, solid green or green with white stripes, and may have spines along the edges. The leaves form a rosette with a cuplike center that can hold water. When the plant matures, flowers emerge from the center of the rosette. The plant dies within two years of flowering.

Selected species and varieties. *N. carolinae,* blushing bromeliad: has solid green leaves 12 inches long. When flowers bloom, the bases of the leaves turn bright red. Flowers are blue or violet. 'Tricolor', striped blushing bromeliad, has bright green leaves striped lengthwise with cream. *N. × marmorata,* marble plant: has leaves 16 inches long and 2½ inches wide that are mottled with purple. Leaf tips are red.

Growing conditions. Blushing bromeliad and marble plant need bright to direct light, an average temperature and medium to high humidity. The potting medium can be kept relatively dry and the water cup in the center of the rosette should be filled with fresh water. Fertilizer can be applied once a month throughout the year. Blushing bromeliad and marble plant can be propagated from offsets and repotted in a peat-based soilless mix.

Blushing bromeliad and marble plant can be damaged by mealybugs and scale insects. They are susceptible to root rot.

Nephrolepis (ne-FROL-e-pis)
Sword fern

Erect fern to 2 feet in height with arching, compound green fronds from 1 to 6 feet long. Slender, furry runners sprout from rhizomes, or underground stems, and root along the surface of the soil.

Selected species and varieties. *N. exaltata:* has feathery, triangular fronds to 6 feet long and 4 inches wide. Fronds are composed of small leaflets with wavy edges. 'Bostoniensis', Boston fern, has a compact form with bright green fronds that grow to 4 feet in length. 'Dallas' has feathery leaflets on fronds that grow to 2 feet in length. 'Fluffy Ruffles' has stiff, dark green fronds that grow erect to 12 inches in height.

Growing conditions. Give sword ferns limited to bright light, average room temperature and high humidity.

Keep the soil evenly moist; if the roots dry out, the fronds will turn brown and may die. Fertilize infrequently; once in spring and once in summer is adequate. Propagate by simple layering of the runners or by division.

Sword ferns can be damaged by scale insects, thrips and whiteflies.

Nephthytis see *Syngonium*

Nertera (ner-TEER-a)

Ground-hugging green plant to 3 inches tall. Thin stems, 12 inches long, grow along the surface of the soil. The stems are covered with tiny oval or rounded leaves ¼ inch in size. Inconspicuous greenish white flowers bloom in summer.

Selected species and varieties. *N. granadensis,* also known as *N. depressa,* bead plant: forms a mound of bright green, rounded leaves. Flowers are followed by glossy bright orange berries.

Growing conditions. Provide bead plant with bright light, a cool temperature and high humidity. Clip with scissors to keep the plant compact. Allow the soil to dry to the touch between thorough waterings. Fertilize only after the plant has flowered in summer; excess fertilizer encourages foliage growth but inhibits flower and fruit production. Propagate by division and use an all-purpose soil mix for repotting.

Bead plant is generally insect- and disease-free.

Norfolk Island pine
see *Araucaria*

Old man cactus
see *Cephalocereus*

Opuntia (oh-PUN-cha)
Cholla, prickly pear cactus

Genus of approximately 300 green cacti, prostrate or erect, several feet tall. The stems are divided into segments that may be flat or cylindrical and that may or may not be covered with spines.

Selected species and varieties. *O. microdasys,* rabbit-ears: grows to 3 feet tall in jointed segments of flat, oval pads. The pads are light green and covered with spots of short, bright yellow bristles. 'Albispina' has white bristles. *O. vulgaris:* has oblong, bright green pads covered with short spines that are pink at the base. 'Variegata' has pads mottled with greenish white.

Growing conditions. Cholla requires direct light, average to warm room temperature, good air circulation and low humidity. It needs little water. Fertilizer can be applied once every other month in spring and summer. Cholla is propagated by removing a pad segment from the cactus and planting it in a cactus mix. The pads should be handled with care; their bristles can work their way into the skin and may be difficult to remove.

Cholla can be damaged by mealybugs and scale insects.

—

Orange see *Citrus*

—

Pandanus (pan-DAY-nus)
Screw pine

Genus of over 650 tropical shrubs and trees that can grow to 60 feet tall in their native habitat. All bear crowns of stiff, leathery, sword-shaped green leaves. Only one species is commonly grown as a houseplant. Screw pines are not related to the true pine genus, *Pinus*.

Selected species and varieties. *P. utilis,* common screw pine: has leaves to 6 feet long and 4 inches wide with prominent red spines along the margins. *P. veitchii,* Veitch screw pine: grows upright to 3 feet tall on a woody stem that bears a rosette of leaves. Leaves are 3 feet long, 3 inches wide, finely toothed on the edges and have narrow yellow or white vertical stripes. 'Compacta' grows to only 18 inches in height. Leaves have prominent white stripes along the edges.

Growing conditions. Screw pines require bright light in summer and direct light in winter. They can also be grown under fluorescent light. They need average room temperature and medium to high humidity. The soil can be allowed to dry moderately between thorough waterings. Fertilizer should be applied just once a year, in late spring. Screw pines can be propagated from offsets that form at the base of the stem. An all-purpose soil mix can be used for repotting.

Screw pines are susceptible to aphids, mealybugs, scale insects, spider mites and thrips.

Panda plant see *Kalanchoe*
Papaya see *Carica*
Parachute plant see *Ceropegia*
Parlor palm see *Chamaedorea*
Partridge breast see *Aloe*
Peacock plant see *Calathea*

—

Pedilanthus (ped-i-LAN-thus)

Upright shrubby succulent that grows to 6 feet in height. Fleshy green stems grow straight or in a zigzag fashion. Leaves are oval and medium green splashed with yellow or white.

Selected species and varieties. *P. tithymaloides,* devil's backbone: grows to 3 feet with zigzagging stems. Leaves are 4 inches long and 2 inches wide. 'Variegatus' grows to 2 feet tall. Leaves are green and yellow and can be flushed with pink.

Growing conditions. Provide direct light, warm room temperature and low humidity. Allow the soil to dry between waterings; too much water can cause stem rot. Fertilize once a month during spring and summer. Propagate from stem cuttings. Avoid contact with the milky sap that runs from the cut end of a stem; the sap can cause skin irritations. Allow the ends of the cuttings to dry for several days before planting. Use a cactus mix for potting.

Devil's backbone can be damaged by mealybugs or spider mites.

—

Pelargonium (pel-ar-GO-nee-um)
Geranium

Genus of about 280 annual or perennial green plants that grow to 5 feet, some cascading, others erect. Leaves may be scalloped, heart-shaped, oval or rounded, furry or smooth and scented or unscented. Small flowers may be white, salmon, red or pink.

Selected species and varieties. *P. graveolens,* rose geranium, sweet-scented geranium: grows erect to 30 inches in height. Leaves are gray-green, deeply cleft, hairy and 2½ inches long. They exude a rose fragrance when touched. *P. tomentosum,* peppermint geranium: grows erect when young and then trails to 2½ feet in length. Leaves are bright green, heart-shaped, velvety and 3 inches long. Leaves exude a strong peppermint fragrance when

PANDANUS UTILIS

PEDILANTHUS TITHYMALOIDES

PELARGONIUM TOMENTOSUM

PELLAEA ROTUNDIFOLIA

PELLIONIA DAVEAUANA

PEPEROMIA OBTUSIFOLIA 'VARIEGATA'

touched. Flower clusters are white or pale pink.

Growing conditions. Geranium needs direct light, average room temperature and medium humidity. The soil should be allowed to dry between thorough waterings; overwatering can foster mildew and rot. Fertilizer can be applied regularly during spring and summer. Geranium can be propagated from stem cuttings and repotted in an all-purpose soil mix. Spent flowers and yellowed leaves should be removed, and leggy stems can be pinched back to encourage full, bushy growth.

Geranium is susceptible to aphids, mealybugs, spider mites and whiteflies. It can also get bacterial leaf and stem blight, edema, powdery mildew and stem rot.

—

Pellaea (pel-LEE-a)

Bushy, upright or trailing green fern to 30 inches. Fronds are compound and grow on wiry stalks that arise from underground stems known as rhizomes.

Selected species and varieties. *P. rotundifolia*, button fern: grows in a trailing manner to a length of 12 inches. Fronds bear pairs of small, rounded, bright green leaves along furry brown midribs.

Growing conditions. Give button fern limited to bright light or grow it under fluorescent light, in a terrarium or in a hanging basket. Provide a cool to average temperature and medium humidity. Keep the soil medium moist; allow it to dry slightly between waterings. Fertilize once a month throughout the year. Propagate by division and pot in a fern mix.

Button fern is vulnerable to aphids, mealybugs and scale insects.

—

Pellionia (pel-ee-O-nee-a)

Trailing green plant to 36 inches in length. Leaves are oval, green and 2½ inches long. Stems may be pink or purple.

Selected species and varieties. *P. daveauana*, trailing watermelon begonia: grows to 2 feet long. Leaves are narrow and oblong. They may be pale or olive green; in either case they have dark green veins and greenish purple margins. Stems are pinkish purple. *P. pulchra*, satin pellionia: has deep green, oval leaves to 2 inches long. Upper surfaces of leaves have dark green veins; under-

sides are flushed with purple. Stems are purple and grow to 18 inches long.

Growing conditions. Trailing watermelon begonia and satin pellionia do best in bright light, average to warm room temperature and medium humidity. They will also thrive under fluorescent light. The soil should be kept evenly moist but not wet and soggy. Fertilizer can be applied regularly in spring and summer. Trailing watermelon begonia and satin pellionia can be propagated by simple layering or from stem cuttings. An all-purpose soil mix can be used for repotting.

Trailing watermelon begonia and satin pellonia are susceptible to mealybugs, scale insects, spider mites and whiteflies.

—

Pencil tree see *Euphorbia*

—

Peperomia (pep-e-RO-mee-a)

Leafy green plant that grows erect to 12 inches or trailing to several feet in length. Leafstalks are fleshy and from 1 to 10 inches long. Leaves are solid green or variegated, quilted or smooth, heart-shaped, oval, rounded or narrow, and grow to 5 inches long. Flower spikes to 10 inches long are produced throughout the year and may be white, cream or green.

Selected species and varieties. *P. argyreia*, watermelon peperomia: grows upright to 12 inches tall. Leaves are 5 inches long and pointed at the tips. They are thick, waxy and dark green with silver lines that resemble the markings on a watermelon rind. Flower spikes are white and about 3 inches long. *P. caperata*, emerald ripple peperomia: grows compact and bushy in a mounded shape to 6 inches high. Leaves are heart-shaped and have a wrinkled texture. They are deep green on the upper surfaces and pale gray-green on the undersides. Flower spikes are white and about 4 inches long.

P. obtusifolia, baby rubber plant: grows compact and bushy to 8 inches high and has oval leaves to 3 inches long. Flower spikes are white and about 3 inches long. 'Variegata' has medium green leaves with cream or yellow margins; some leaves are completely yellow. *P. orba*, pixie peperomia: grows in a compact, mounded form on hairy stems to 7 inches long. Leaves are oval and glossy green with faint gray mottling. Undersides are velvety gray-green. The plant sometimes produces

124

creamy white flower spikes up to 6 inches in length. *P. scandens*, philodendron peperomia: grows in a climbing or trailing manner to several feet long. Leaves are light green, heart-shaped and up to 3 inches long. Flowers are rarely produced indoors. 'Variegata' has light green leaves with cream margins.

Growing conditions. Variegated peperomias do best in bright light; solid-colored varieties need limited to bright light and protection from the summer sun. Insufficient light can cause stems to become weak and spindly. Peperomias need average to warm room temperature and medium to high humidity. The soil should be allowed to dry between waterings; too much water can cause the leaves to drop. Emerald ripple peperomia is especially sensitive to overwatering and can develop crown or stem rot. Fertilizer should be applied once a month in spring and summer. Peperomias can be propagated from leaf and stem cuttings and by division. An all-purpose soil mix can be used for potting.

Peperomia is susceptible to mealybugs, spider mites and whiteflies. It can develop edema and root and stem rot.

—

Peppermint geranium
see *Pelargonium*

—

Persea (PUR-see-a)

Genus of about 150 tropical trees that grow to over 60 feet tall in their native habitat. Only one species is grown as a houseplant.

Selected species and varieties. *P. americana*, avocado: grows 4 to 6 feet in height on an erect, single stem. Leaves are dark green, leathery, elliptic and grow from 4 to 8 inches in length. Fruit is not produced indoors.

Growing conditions. Give avocado direct light; insufficient light will cause spindly growth. Provide a warm temperature and medium humidity. Keep the soil evenly moist but not wet and soggy. Fertilize once a month throughout the year. Propagate from seeds saved from fresh, store-bought avocados. Use an all-purpose soil mix for repotting. Mature plants may require staking.

Avocado is vulnerable to aphids, mealybugs, scale insects and thrips.

Persian shield see *Strobilanthes*
Petticoat palm see *Washingtonia*

—

Philodendron (fil-o-DEN-dron)

Climbing, trailing or occasionally erect tropical green plant with thick stems to 6 feet in length. Leaves may be green or red, and heart-shaped, fiddle-shaped, sword-shaped, rounded or triangular. They may have smooth edges or deep clefts.

Selected species and varieties. *P. bipennifolium*, horsehead philodendron: has deeply cleft, triangular, glossy green leaves approximately 15 inches long. *P.* × 'Burgundy': has narrow, triangular leaves 12 inches long. Leaves are bright red when new and turn green as they mature. The undersides of the leaves remain burgundy. Stems and leafstalks are red. *P. erubescens*, redleaf philodendron: has shiny, dark green, triangular leaves up to 10 inches in length. Undersides of leaves are coppery red. Stems and leafstalks are red.
P. pinnatilobum 'Fernleaf', fernleaf philodendron: has medium green, finely cut leaves that resemble fern fronds. *P. scandens oxycardium*, heart-leaf philodendron: is a trailing vine several feet long with small, heart-shaped leaves to 4 inches in length. Leaves emerge bronze and turn green as they mature. *P. selloum*, tree philodendron: grows erect to 6 feet tall on a trunklike stem. Leaves are glossy green, deeply cleft and 18 inches long.

Growing conditions. Philodendron does best in bright light; limited light may cause small leaves and straggly growth. It needs an average to warm temperature and medium humidity. The soil should be allowed to dry to the touch between thorough waterings; overwatering can cause brown spots to form on the leaves and root rot. The leaves can be rinsed or sponged with water often to keep them clean and glossy. Fertilizer should be applied regularly during spring and summer. Climbing philodendrons need a support, such as a piece of bark or a moss-covered pole. Philodendrons can be propagated from stem cuttings, by air layering and by simple layering. They can be potted in an all-purpose soil mix.

Philodendron is vulnerable to aphids, mealybugs, scale insects and spider mites. It is also susceptible to bacterial leaf spot, root rot and salt buildup.

PERSEA AMERICANA

PHILODENDRON SCANDENS OXYCARDIUM

PHOENIX ROEBELENII

PILEA CADIEREI

PISONIA UMBELLIFERA 'VARIEGATA'

Phoenix (FEE-nix)
Date palm

Tropical palm to 6 feet in height. Fronds are compound and grow to 3 feet long from a thick, brown base.

Selected species and varieties. *P. roebelenii,* miniature date palm: grows to 4 feet tall and has delicate, arching, dark green fronds.

Growing conditions. Date palm can be grown in bright light or under fluorescent light. It needs medium humidity, a warm temperature by day and a slightly cooler temperature at night. The soil should be kept relatively dry. Fertilizer should be applied regularly during spring and summer. Commercially, date palm is propagated from seed under special greenhouse conditions; home propagation from seed is not recommended. Occasionally, offsets arise from the base of date palms grown indoors; these offsets can be used for propagation. An all-purpose soil mix can be used for potting. Date palm is a slow grower and needs repotting only once every three years or when roots appear along the surface of the soil.

Date palm is vulnerable to attack by mealybugs, scale insects and spider mites.

—

Piggyback plant see *Tolmiea*

—

Pilea (py-LEE-a)

Compact, bushy green plant that grows erect to 12 inches tall or forms a low mound to 12 inches wide. Stems are fleshy and bear green leaves marked with silver, brown, bronze or red. Leaves may be puckered or smooth and ¼ inch to 3 inches long.

Selected species and varieties. *P. acuminata:* has a mounded, compact shape and grows to 8 inches in height. 'Moon Valley' has leaves that are 3 inches long with a quilted texture. Upper surfaces are bright green with brown veins and brown stripes along the center ribs. *P. cadierei,* aluminum plant: grows erect to 12 inches tall. Leaves are 3 inches long and light green with raised silver patches. *P. microphylla,* artillery plant: grows to 10 inches tall in a mounded shape with spreading stems. Tiny leaves about ¼ inch long form in clusters that resemble feathery fern foliage. Artillery plant got its name because it expels its pollen in a strong spray. *P. nummulariifolia,* creeping Charlie: grows in a ground-hugging form and has thin, reddish branches to 10 inches long. Leaves are pale green, rounded, ¾ inch wide and have a quilted surface. *P. spruceana:* grows in either a creeping or an upright form. 'Norfolk', angelwings, grows in a creeping habit and forms tight rosettes of cross-paired, circular leaves. Leaves are from 1½ to 3 inches wide and bronze with raised silver stripes. 'Silver Tree' grows upright to 10 inches tall and has hairy white leafstalks. Leaves are 3 inches long and greenish bronze with wide silver stripes and silver dots. Undersides are covered with reddish hairs.

Growing conditions. Give pileas limited to bright light, warm room temperature and medium to high humidity. Allow the soil to dry to the touch between thorough waterings. Fertilize regularly in spring and summer. Pinch back the mound-forming varieties regularly to maintain full, dense growth. Propagate from stem cuttings and pot in an all-purpose soil mix.

Artillery plant, 'Moon Valley' and creeping Charlie are all suitable for hanging baskets.

Pileas are vulnerable to mealybugs, scale insects and root rot.

—

Pineapple see *Ananas*

—

Pisonia (pi-ZO-nee-a)

Upright tropical shrubs and small trees with oblong, leathery green leaves to 15 inches in length. Leaves grow in pairs along the stems. Only one species is grown as a houseplant.

Selected species and varieties. *P. umbellifera,* also known as *Heimerliodendron brunonianum,* bird-catcher tree: grows to 4 feet in height. Leaves are bright green and sticky along the center. 'Variegata' has cream or yellow patches along the leaf margins.

Growing conditions. Bird-catcher tree needs bright to direct light to maintain its best leaf coloration. It does best in warm room temperature and medium to high humidity. The soil should be allowed to dry to the touch between thorough waterings. Fertilizer can be applied once a month during spring and summer. Bird-catcher tree can be propagated from stem cuttings, and an all-purpose soil mix can be used for potting.

Bird-catcher tree is relatively free

of insects and diseases; it is susceptible to damage from spider mites.

—

Pitcher plant see *Sarracenia*

—

Pittosporum (pi-TOS-po-rum)

Tropical evergreen shrub or tree that can grow to 60 feet tall in its native habitat. Species grown indoors rarely reach more than 5 feet in height. Clusters of green, purple or variegated leaves sprout from the branch tips.

Selected species and varieties. *P. tobira,* Australian laurel, Japanese pittosporum: grows in a shrublike form. Erect, branching stems produce whorls of glossy, leathery, narrow green leaves 4 inches long and 1 inch wide. 'Variegata' has bright green leaves with white or cream edges.

Growing conditions. Australian laurel does best in bright light, a cool temperature and low to medium humidity; it can tolerate a warm temperature if the humidity is increased. The soil should be kept relatively dry. Australian laurel should be fertilized once in spring and once in summer. The foliage should be rinsed regularly to keep it clean and glossy. Australian laurel can be propagated from stem cuttings. Since it is a slow grower, a rooting hormone should be used to promote root development. An all-purpose soil mix can be used for potting.

Australian laurel is vulnerable to attack by aphids, mealybugs, mites and scale insects.

—

Platycerium (plat-i-SEER-ee-um)

Epiphytic tropical fern with a flat frond at its base; the frond covers the roots, which will cling to a support. Compound green fronds in the shape of deer antlers grow from the base.

Selected species and varieties. *P. bifurcatum,* staghorn fern: produces broad, gray-green fronds that may be erect or drooping. The deeply cleft fronds grow to 3 feet wide and 1 to 2 feet long. The base frond is green and felty when young and turns dry and brown as it ages. New base fronds grow over mature ones.

Growing conditions. Staghorn fern needs bright light, good air circulation, warm room temperature and high humidity. It does best mounted on a support, such as a slab

of tree bark with sphagnum moss around the base. It can be watered regularly by submerging the bark slab in a sink or a container of water for about five minutes or until the medium is thoroughly wet. Staghorn fern may also be grown in a pot filled with half sphagnum moss and half peat-based soilless mix. It can be propagated from offsets that arise at the base of the plant.

Staghorn fern is free of most insects and diseases, but is susceptible to damage by scale insects.

—

Plectranthus (plek-TRAN-thus)
Swedish ivy

Shrublike or trailing green plant with fleshy, square stems that grow to 3 feet long. Stems bear green leaves that may be heart-shaped, oval or rounded and grow to 2½ inches in length. Leaves emit a distinctive odor when bruised.

Selected species and varieties. *P. australis:* trails to 2 feet in length and has shiny, dark green rounded leaves. Small flowers are light blue. *P. coleoides:* trails to 3 feet in length and has furry, heart-shaped gray-green leaves on purple stems. 'Marginatus', white-edged Swedish ivy, has leaves with white edges.

Growing conditions. Swedish ivy does best in bright light, an average temperature and medium humidity. It can also grow in a warm temperature if the humidity is increased. The soil can be allowed to dry moderately between thorough waterings. Fertilizer should be applied regularly in spring and summer. The stems can be pinched back frequently to encourage full, bushy growth. The trailing forms of Swedish ivy are suitable for planting in hanging baskets. Swedish ivy can be propagated from stem cuttings and repotted in an all-purpose soil mix.

Swedish ivy can get aphids, mealybugs and whiteflies.

—

Pleomele (plee-O-ma-lee)

Shrubby plant from 20 inches to 10 feet tall. Stems are woody. Narrow, pointed leaves grow to 1 foot long. They may be solid green or green with stripes or spots.

Selected species and varieties. *P. reflexa,* also known as *Dracaena reflexa:* has dark green leaves that are slightly arched. 'Variegata,' Song of India, has leaves with light green centers and creamy yellow margins.

PITTOSPORUM TOBIRA 'VARIEGATA'

PLATYCERIUM BIFURCATUM

PLECTRANTHUS AUSTRALIS

PLEOMELE REFLEXA 'VARIEGATA'

PODOCARPUS MACROPHYLLUS

POLYPODIUM AUREUM

POLYSCIAS FRUTICOSA

Growing Conditions. Provide Song of India with bright light, average temperature and medium to high humidity. Keep the soil moderately dry and fertilize once every three months in spring and summer. Stake Song of India if it gets top-heavy or prune it to grow in a spreading form. Propagate by air layering or from stem cuttings and offsets. Use an all-purpose soil mix for repotting.

Song of India is generally insect- and disease-free.

—

Podocarpus (po-doh-KAR-pus)

Genus of approximately 75 species of evergreen shrubs and trees that can grow to 100 feet in their native habitat. Only one species is grown as a houseplant.

Selected species and varieties. *P. macrophyllus,* Buddhist pine: is a bushy shrub that grows to 5 feet in height with upright woody stems. Leaves are narrow, dark green and from 2 to 4 inches long.

Growing conditions. Give Buddhist pine bright light or grow it under fluorescent light. Provide a cool to average temperature and medium humidity. Allow the soil to dry moderately between thorough waterings. Fertilize twice a year, once in spring and once in summer. Repot Buddhist pine only when it outgrows its container and use an all-purpose soil mix for potting. Propagate from woody stem cuttings. A rooting hormone should be used to promote root growth.

Buddhist pine is susceptible to damage from scale insects and spider mites.

—

Polka-dot plant see *Hypoestes*

—

Polypodium (pol-i-PO-dee-um)

Epiphytic fern with furry, rust-colored stems called rhizomes that grow along the surface of the soil and resemble rabbits' feet. Green fronds to 30 inches in length grow from 2-foot-long stalks attached to the stems. The fronds are triangular in shape and may be deeply cleft, lobed or ruffled.

Selected species and varieties. *P. aureum,* hare's-foot fern: has thin, deeply cleft, light green fronds 2 feet in length.

Growing conditions. Hare's-foot fern can be grown in bright light or

under fluorescent light. It does best in average room temperature with high humidity. The soil should be allowed to dry to the touch between thorough waterings. Fertilizer can be applied monthly throughout the year. Hare's-foot fern can be propagated by dividing the rhizomes and potted in a fern mix.

Hare's-foot fern is vulnerable to attack by aphids, mealybugs and scale insects.

—

Polyscias (po-LIS-ee-as)

Genus of upright shrubs or trees that grow to several feet tall. Stems are woody and bear leaves that may be green or variegated, solid or finely divided, and from 3 to 15 inches long.

Selected species and varieties. *P. balfouriana,* Balfour aralia: grows to 6 feet in height on woody green stems with gray speckles. Leaves are glossy dark green and shell-shaped with scalloped edges. As leaves mature, they become divided into three sections. 'Marginata' has gray-green leaves with jagged white edges. *P. fruticosa,* ming aralia: grows in a treelike form to 4 feet tall. A single woody stem bears purple-green leafstalks and lacy, finely divided green leaves. *P. guilfoylei,* geranium leaf aralia, grows to 3 feet tall. Leaves are oval, 16 inches long, lacy and bright green. 'Victoriae' has slightly smaller leaves with white edges. *P. paniculata:* grows to 4 feet tall in a shrublike form. Leaves are willowy and shiny dark green. 'Variegata', variegated aralia: has leaves variegated dark and light green with white markings.

Growing conditions. Aralias need bright light, warm room temperature and high humidity. The soil should be allowed to dry to the touch between waterings; wet soil can foster root rot. Fertilizer can be applied once a month from early spring through late fall. Aralias can be propagated from stem cuttings and repotted in an all-purpose soil mix.

Aralias are vulnerable to aphids, mealybugs, scale insects and spider mites. They can also get root rot.

—

Ponytail see *Beaucarnea*

Pothos see *Epipremnum; Scindapsus*

Powder puff cactus see *Mammillaria*

Prayer plant see *Maranta*

Prickly pear cactus see *Opuntia*

Pteris (TEER-is)
Table fern

Small, upright fern to 20 inches in height. Stalks are blackish or green and bear solid green or striped fronds to 24 inches long and 12 inches wide.

Selected species and varieties. *P. cretica*, Cretan brake fern: has black stalks with narrow, straplike bright green leaflets to 12 inches in length. *P. ensiformis*: has triangular fronds to 20 inches long and narrow leaflets. 'Victoriae', silver-leaf fern, has silver-white leaflets with green margins. *P. quadriaurita*: has divided fronds up to 3 feet long and 1½ feet wide on wiry black stems. 'Argyraea', silver-lace fern, has a silver midrib.

Growing conditions. Give table fern limited to bright light or grow it under fluorescent light. Provide an average temperature and medium humidity. Keep the soil evenly moist but not wet and soggy. Fertilize once a month during spring and summer. Propagate by division of the roots and use a fern mix for repotting.

Table fern can be damaged by aphids, mealybugs, scale insects and root rot.

—

Purple passion vine see *Gynura*

Purple velvet plant see *Gynura*

Purple waffle plant
see *Hemigraphis*

Queen's umbrella tree
see *Brassaia*

Rabbit-ears see *Opuntia*

Rabbit's-foot fern see *Davallia*

—

Radermachera
(rod-er-MOK-er-a)

Evergreen shrub or tree that grows to several feet in height on a woody stem. Leaves are green and may be oblong or oval. Only one species is grown as a houseplant.

Selected species and varieties. *R. sinica*, China doll: grows to 4 feet in height. Leafstalks are long and bear glossy deep green leaves with light green undersides. Leaves are lobed, about 2 inches long and 1 inch wide.

Growing conditions. China doll does best in direct light, average room temperature and medium humidity. It can tolerate fluctuations in temperature. The soil should be kept evenly moist; if it dries, the leaves may wither and drop. Fertilize regu-

larly in spring and summer. Repot in an all-purpose soil mix.

Commercially, China doll is propagated under special greenhouse conditions; home propagation is not recommended.

China doll is susceptible to damage from aphids, mealybugs, scale insects and whiteflies.

—

Rattail see *Aporocactus; Crassula*

Red-nerve plant see *Fittonia*

—

Rhapis (RAY-pis)
Lady palm

Reedlike palm that grows to 5 feet in height in clumps of stiff stems. It has fronds that are fan-shaped and divided lengthwise into narrow green leaves that may be blunt-edged or pointed.

Selected species and varieties. *R. excelsa*, slender lady palm: has shiny bright green fronds divided into five to eight leaves up to 9 inches long and 2 inches wide.

Growing conditions. Give lady palm limited light, average room temperature and low humidity. Allow the potting medium to dry moderately between thorough waterings. Sponge, rinse or shower the foliage regularly to remove dirt and dust. Fertilize once a month during spring and summer. Propagate by division or from offsets and repot in a peat-based soilless mix.

Lady palm can be damaged by mealybugs, scale insects and spider mites.

—

Rhoeo (REE-o)

Upright green plant that forms rosettes of stiff, dagger-shaped green leaves to 12 inches tall.

Selected species and varieties. *R. spathacea*, also known as *R. discolor*, Moses-in-the-cradle: leaves are purple at the base and have purple undersides. Small white flowers bloom inside pink bracts that resemble boats. 'Variegata' has bright yellow vertical stripes.

Growing conditions. Moses-in-the-cradle needs bright light, an average temperature and medium to high humidity. The soil should be allowed to dry between waterings. Fertilizer can be applied regularly during spring and summer. Moses-in-the-cradle can be propagated from offsets and repotted in an all-purpose soil mix.

PTERIS QUADRIAURITA 'ARGYRAEA'

RADERMACHERA SINICA

RHAPIS EXCELSA

RHOEO SPATHACEA

129

SANSEVIERIA TRIFASCIATA 'LAURENTII'

SARRACENIA PURPUREA

SAXIFRAGA STOLONIFERA

Moses-in-the-cradle is susceptible to mealybugs and spider mites.

—

Rock foil see *Saxifraga*
Rosary vine see *Ceropegia*
Rose geranium see *Pelargonium*
Rubber ivy see *Senecio*
Rubber plant see *Ficus*
Sago palm see *Cycas*
Sand dollar cactus
see *Astrophytum*

—

Sansevieria (san-se-VEER-ee-a)
Snake plant, good luck plant

Fleshy, stiff-leaved succulent that may be erect to 3 feet tall or low-growing, in rosettes, to a few inches in height. Leaves can be solid green or variegated.

Selected species and varieties. *S. trifasciata:* has narrow, sword-shaped leaves that grow to 3 feet long and are marked with bands of light and dark green. 'Hahnii', bird's-nest sansevieria, forms squat rosettes of leaves to 6 inches in height. 'Laurentii', mother-in-law's tongue, has erect, leathery, sword-shaped leaves to 36 inches tall. Leaves may be gray-green or dark green with yellow margins and irregular horizontal bands of silver, light green or black-green. Leaf edges tend to curl.

Growing conditions. Snake plant does best in bright to direct light, an average to warm temperature and medium humidity. It can adapt to a wide range of conditions, but limited light and low humidity can slow its growth. The soil should be allowed to dry between waterings; overwatering can foster root rot. It should be fertilized every other month during spring and summer. It can be propagated from offsets, leaf section cuttings and by division of the roots. Snake plant needs repotting only when it outgrows its container. Half cactus mix and half all-purpose mix should be used for repotting.

Snake plant can be damaged by mealybugs and scale insects. It is susceptible to leaf and root rot.

—

Sarracenia (sar-a-SEE-nee-a)
Pitcher plant

Carnivorous bog plant that grows from 6 to 24 inches tall from underground stems called rhizomes.

Leaves form hollow tubes with short, soft hairs on the edges, and may be green, purple or red flushed with yellow. The lip of each leaf secretes a nectar that attracts insects; insects fall into a watery pool at the bottom of the leaf and are digested by the plant. Flowers bloom in spring or summer and are greenish purple to wine red, umbrella-like and slightly drooping.

Selected species and varieties. *S. purpurea,* common pitcher plant: grows to 6 inches tall. Leaves are green and flushed with brownish purple. Leaf edges and veins are red.

Growing conditions. Pitcher plant needs bright to direct light, a cool temperature, high humidity and a constantly moist growing medium; it does best in a terrarium. Sphagnum moss should be used for a planting medium. If pitcher plant does not catch insects, it should be fertilized once a week during spring and summer. It can be propagated by division of its rhizomes and from seed. Seeds should be placed in a moist paper towel in the refrigerator for six weeks to activate their growth.

Pitcher plant is not susceptible to insect damage, since it consumes them. It is also disease-free.

—

Saxifraga (saks-IF-ra-ga)
Rock foil

Genus of approximately 300 species of low-growing, stemless green plants. Leaves form in rosette-shaped clusters on a central base that grows from underground stems called rhizomes. Only one species is grown as a houseplant.

Selected species and varieties. *S. stolonifera,* strawberry begonia: grows to 6 inches tall. Leaves are rounded with scalloped edges. Upper surfaces are olive green streaked with silver; undersides are reddish. Leaves and leafstalks are covered with fine, greenish hairs. Tiny plantlets are produced at the ends of long, trailing stems.

Growing conditions. Give strawberry begonia bright light, average room temperature and medium humidity. Allow the soil to become moderately dry between thorough waterings. Fertilize once a month during spring and summer. Propagate from plantlets and use an all-purpose soil mix for repotting.

Strawberry begonia can be attacked by aphids, mealybugs and whiteflies. It is also susceptible to salt buildup.

Schefflera see *Brassaia; Schefflera*

—

Schefflera (shef-LEER-a)

Tropical evergreen shrub that grows to 5 feet in height.

Selected species and varieties. *S. arboricola,* also known as *Heptapleurum arboricola,* dwarf schefflera: has shiny, leathery green leaves. Each leaf is composed of seven to nine leaflets arranged in a circle on a slender leafstalk. The leaflets are narrow and oval, and grow to 5 inches long. 'Variegata' has pale yellow blotches.

Growing conditions. Dwarf schefflera does best in bright light, average room temperature and medium to high humidity. The soil should be allowed to dry to the touch between thorough waterings; wet soil can cause leaves to drop. Fertilize regularly from early spring through late autumn. Dwarf schefflera can be propagated from stem cuttings and repotted in an all-purpose soil mix.

Dwarf schefflera is vulnerable to damage by mealybugs, scale insects and whiteflies.

—

Scindapsus (sin-DAP-sus)

Tropical vining plant that trails or climbs to 40 feet in its natural habitat. Leaves are rounded. Leaves form on rounded green stems and may be heart-shaped or oval.

Selected species and varieties. *S. pictus:* grows to 6 feet in length. Leaves are heart-shaped, 2 to 3 inches long and dark green marbled with silver. 'Argyraeus', satin pothos, has olive green leaves with silver spots.

Growing conditions. Satin pothos can be grown in bright light or under fluorescent light. It needs average room temperature and medium humidity. Temperatures below 60° F can damage the foliage and cause the leaves to curl. The soil should be allowed to dry to the touch between thorough waterings. Fertilizer can be applied two or three times during spring and summer. Pothos can be propagated throughout the year from stem cuttings or by simple layering. An all-purpose soil mix can be used for repotting. Pothos is suitable for growing in a hanging basket.

Pothos can get mealybugs and spider mites.

Screw pine see *Pandanus*

Sea urchin cactus
see *Astrophytum*

—

Sedum (SEE-dum)
Stonecrop

Trailing or erect shrubby succulent to several feet. Fleshy leaves sprout directly from thick, branching stems.

Selected species and varieties. *S. morganianum,* burro's tail: has trailing stems that dangle to 3 feet. The stems are obscured by layers of loosely attached, thick, tear-shaped, gray-green leaves ¾ inch long.

Growing conditions. Give burro's tail direct light, average to warm room temperature and medium humidity. Let the soil dry moderately between waterings. Do not fertilize burro's tail; it makes efficient use of available nutrients in the soil and the addition of fertilizer may burn the plant. Propagate by division or from leaf or stem cuttings. Let the stem cuttings dry before planting. Use a cactus mix for repotting. Handle the plant with care; leaves are easily dislodged or knocked off, which creates bald areas on the stem. Burro's tail is suitable for a hanging basket.

Burro's tail is susceptible to mealybugs and scale insects.

—

Selaginella (sel-a-ji-NELL-a)

Mossy, fernlike green plant that grows in mounded clumps or upright with creeping branches to 2 feet long.

Selected species and varieties. *S. kraussiana,* spreading club moss: grows in low mounds to 12 inches wide. Tiny, bright green leaves that resemble scales grow along creeping stems; the stems root as they spread across the surface of the soil.

Growing conditions. Spreading club moss needs limited light, a warm temperature, high humidity and an evenly moist potting medium; the leaves will wither and the plant may die in hot, dry conditions. It does well in a dish garden or a terrarium. Fertilizer should be applied regularly throughout the year. Spreading club moss can be propagated by division. It should be planted in a peat-based soilless mix.

Spreading club moss is generally insect- and disease-free, but leaf damage can occur if cold water is used to moisten the soil; lukewarm water should be used.

SCHEFFLERA ARBORICOLA 'VARIEGATA'

SCINDAPSUS PICTUS 'ARGYRAEUS'

SEDUM MORGANIANUM

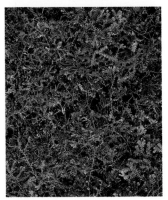

SELAGINELLA KRAUSSIANA

131

SENECIO MACROGLOSSUS 'VARIEGATUM'

SOLEIROLIA SOLEIROLII

STROBILANTHES DYERANUS

Senecio (se-NEE-see-o)

A large genus having more than 2,000 species of widely diverse plants ranging in size from 10 inches to 10 feet. Some are creeping, others are erect; some are solid green, others are variegated.

Selected species and varieties. *S. macroglossus,* rubber ivy: trails to 3 feet in length. Short leafstalks bear 2½-inch-long, arrow-shaped green leaves that resemble ivy leaves. 'Variegatum', variegated rubber ivy: has purple stems and leafstalks. Leaves are green with irregular yellow markings. *S. mikanioides,* German ivy: trails to 3 feet in length. Leaves are dark green, have pointed lobes and grow to 3 inches long. *S. rowleyanus,* string-of-beads: trails to 3 feet and has rounded, pea-sized, light green leaves.

Growing conditions. Variegated rubber ivy needs direct light for best leaf color. Rubber ivy, German ivy and string-of-beads need bright to direct light. All do well in average temperature and medium humidity and are suitable for growing in hanging baskets. The soil for rubber ivy and string-of-beads can be kept relatively dry; German ivy needs evenly moist soil. Fertilize regularly in spring and summer. The stem tips can be pinched back often to promote full, bushy growth. All can be propagated from stem cuttings. Rubber ivy and German ivy can be potted in an all-purpose soil mix; string-of-beads can be potted in a cactus mix.

Rubber ivy, German ivy and string-of-beads are vulnerable to aphids, mealybugs, scale insects and spider mites.

—

Sensitive plant see *Mimosa*

Sentry palm see *Howea*

Setcreasea see *Callisia*

Silk oak tree see *Grevillea*

Silver-lace fern see *Pteris*

Silver-leaf fern see *Pteris*

Silver-nerve plant see *Fittonia*

Silver vase see *Aechmea*

Snake plant see *Sansevieria*

Snowball cactus see *Mammillaria*

—

Soleirolia (so-le-RO-lee-a)

A mat-forming green plant with creeping, fleshy stems that grow to about 6 inches in length. It has tiny green leaves ¼ inch wide.

Selected species and varieties. *S. soleirolii,* baby's tears: has bright green, rounded leaves on short, delicate leafstalks.

Growing conditions. Give baby's tears limited light to bright light; direct sun will burn the leaves. Provide an average temperature, high humidity and evenly moist soil or grow it in a terrarium. Fertilize baby's tears regularly during spring and summer. Clip the foliage with scissors to keep it full and compact. Propagate by division and use an all-purpose soil mix for potting.

Baby's tears is not generally bothered by insects or diseases.

—

Song of India see *Pleomele*

Spanish bayonet see *Yucca*

Spanish moss see *Tillandsia*

Spider flower see *Grevillea*

Spider plant see *Chlorophytum*

Spindle tree see *Euonymus*

Split-leaf philodendron see *Monstera*

Spreading club moss see *Selaginella*

Squirrel's-foot fern see *Davallia*

Staghorn fern see *Platycerium*

Star cactus see *Astrophytum*

Stonecrop see *Sedum*

Stone plant see *Lithops*

Strap flower see *Anthurium*

Strawberry begonia see *Saxifraga*

String-of-beads see *Senecio*

String-of-hearts see *Ceropegia*

—

Strobilanthes (stro-bi-LAN-theez)

Upright tropical shrub to 3 feet in height. Only one species is grown as a houseplant.

Selected species and varieties. *S. dyeranus,* Persian shield: grows to 2 feet tall. Stems are furry and bear pairs of narrow, triangular leaves from 6 to 8 inches long. Upper leaf surfaces are dark green flushed with purple and undersides are purple.

Growing conditions. Persian shield requires bright light, average to warm room temperature and high humidity. The soil should be allowed to dry slightly between thorough waterings. Fertilizer can be applied regularly in spring and summer. The stems should be pinched back frequently to encourage full, bushy growth. Persian shield can be propagated from stem cuttings, and a rooting hormone should be used to encourage root development. An all-purpose soil mix can be used for repotting.

Persian shield is relatively free of insects and diseases; it is susceptible to aphids.

—

Sundew see *Drosera*

Swedish ivy see *Plectranthus*

Sweet flag see *Acorus*

Sweet-scented geranium see *Pelargonium*

Swiss cheese plant see *Monstera*

Sword fern see *Nephrolepis*

—

Syngonium (sin-GO-nee-um)

Tropical climbing or trailing vine with fleshy stems that grow to 6 feet in length. Leaves may be green or variegated and from 3 inches to 12 inches long. The leaves change shape as the plant matures; on young plants they are solid and triangular; on older plants they become deeply cleft, forming from three to nine leaflets.

Selected species and varieties. *S. podophyllum,* formerly known as *Nephthytis,* arrowhead vine: has lustrous, medium green leaves, often variegated with white or yellow.

Growing conditions. Give arrowhead plant bright light, a warm temperature and medium to high humidity. Water moderately and allow the soil to dry between waterings. Fertilize regularly in spring and summer. Propagate from stem cuttings and repot in an all-purpose soil mix.

Arrowhead vine is susceptible to mealybugs, spider mites, bacterial leaf spot and root rot.

—

Table fern see *Pteris*

Tahitian bridal veil see *Gibasis*

Tailflower see *Anthurium*

Teddy bear plant see *Cyanotis*

Ti plant see *Cordyline*

Tiger's jaw see *Faucaria*

—

Tillandsia (til-LAND-zee-a)

Epiphytic bromeliad that may grow in rosettes several feet across or in trailing clumps of stems several feet long; the stems are covered with tiny, scalelike leaves.

Selected species and varieties. *T. caput-Medusae,* Medusa's head: grows to 10 inches tall from a bulbous stem base. Leaves are long, fleshy, straplike and gray to gray-green. Purple flower spikes may be produced between red, pink or green bracts. *T. usneoides,* Spanish moss: has trailing, threadlike stems that bear gray, scalelike leaves. Tiny green flowers that turn yellow with age are sometimes produced indoors.

Growing conditions. Medusa's head and Spanish moss need bright light, warm room temperature and high humidity. Medusa's head can be either anchored to a slab of bark or grown in a pot. If it is grown in a pot, a peat-based soilless mix should be used. Spanish moss can be anchored to tree bark or draped over any structure to hang freely. The planting medium should be kept evenly moist; to water mounted plants, submerge the bark slab in a sink or pail of water, or mist twice a week. Medusa's head can be fertilized once a month throughout the year. Spanish moss uses available nutrients efficiently and needs no fertilizer. Medusa's head can be propagated from offsets. Spanish moss can be propagated by separating entire stem sections from the main plant.

Medusa's head and Spanish moss are susceptible to scale insects.

—

Tolmiea (TOL-mee-a)

One-species genus of compact, mounded green plants to 12 inches tall and 15 inches wide.

Selected species and varieties. *T. menziesii,* piggyback plant: has a short stem with 4-inch-long, hairy leafstalks and hairy, heart-shaped, dark green leaves up to 3 inches wide. Young plantlets form at the base of the leaves.

Growing conditions. Provide piggyback plant with bright light or grow it under fluorescent light. Maintain cool to average room temperature and medium humidity. Allow the soil to dry between waterings; overwatering can cause leaf tip burn. Fer-

SYNGONIUM PODOPHYLLUM

TILLANDSIA CAPUT-MEDUSAE

TOLMIEA MENZIESII

TRADESCANTIA SILLAMONTANA

WASHINGTONIA FILIFERA

YUCCA ALOIFOLIA

tilize regularly in spring and summer. Propagate from plantlets and pot in an all-purpose soil mix.

Piggyback plant can be damaged by mealybugs, spider mites and whiteflies. It is susceptible to powdery mildew and salt buildup.

—

Tradescantia
(trad-e-SKAN-shi-a)

Trailing green plant with fleshy stems that bear pointed oval leaves from 2 to 4 inches long. Small white or pink flowers bloom in spring.

Selected species and varieties. *T. fluminensis,* wandering Jew: grows to 2 feet in length. Upper leaf surfaces are blue-green; undersides are deep purple. Flowers are white. 'Variegata' has leaves with white lengthwise stripes. A few leaves may be solid white or solid green. *T. sillamontana,* white velvet plant: has woolly white hairs on leaves and stems. Leaves are green with purple undersides and grow to 2½ inches long. Flowers are pink-purple.

Growing conditions. Wandering Jew and white velvet plant do best in bright light, an average temperature and medium humidity. The soil should be allowed to dry between thorough waterings; overwatering encourages rot. Fertilizer can be applied regularly from early spring to late fall. Dried leaves should be removed and the stems should be pinched back frequently to encourage full, bushy growth. Wandering Jew and white velvet plant can be propagated from stem cuttings and repotted in an all-purpose soil mix.

Wandering Jew and white velvet plant are susceptible to damage from mealybugs, scale insects, spider mites and whiteflies.

—

Trailing begonia vine
see *Cissus*

Tripogandra see *Gibasis*

Umbrella plant see *Cyperus*

Umbrella tree see *Brassaia*

Venus flytrap see *Dionaea*

Venus's hair see *Adiantum*

Wandering Jew
see *Tradescantia; Zebrina*

Wart plant see *Haworthia*

Washington fan palm
see *Washingtonia*

Washingtonia
(wash-ing-TOH-nee-a)
Washington fan palm

Fan palm tree that grows erect to 6 feet tall. The trunk gives rise to spiny leafstalks 18 to 20 inches long and has short stubs or shingles where old leaves grew. Fronds are cut into many narrow, stiff leaf segments. Shredded brown fibers dangle from the leaf sections.

Selected species and varieties. *W. filifera,* desert fan palm, petticoat palm: grows to 4 feet in height. Fronds are green and arching, with a spread of 2 feet.

Growing conditions. Desert fan palm needs bright light, average room temperature and low to medium humidity. Although it can tolerate dry air, it grows best in a slightly moist environment. It can be placed outdoors in summer to promote good foliage color and growth, provided it is in a location that is protected from scorching sun and fierce winds. The soil should be kept moderately dry. Fertilizer should be applied regularly in spring and summer. Repotting is necessary only when the tree outgrows its container, and an all-purpose soil mix can be used. Commercial growers propagate desert fan palm from seed under special greenhouse conditions; home propagation is not recommended.

Desert fan palm is susceptible to mealybugs, nematodes, scale insects and spider mites.

—

Watermelon begonia
see *Pellionia*

Watermelon peperomia
see *Peperomia*

Wax plant see *Hoya*

West Indian holly see *Leea*

White velvet plant
see *Tradescantia*

Yellow palm see *Chrysalidocarpus*

—

Yucca (YUK-a)

Treelike plant grows to 6 feet tall on a thick, woody trunk. Leaves are green, sword-shaped and grow to 4 feet long.

Selected species and varieties. *Y. aloifolia,* Spanish bayonet: grows to 4 feet tall. Leaves are stiff, have sharp, pointed tips and are about 18 inches long. *Y. elephantipes,* spineless yucca: grows to 6 feet tall and has soft, arching, glossy green leaves to 4 feet long.

Growing conditions. Yucca needs bright to direct light, an average temperature, good air circulation and medium humidity. It can be placed outdoors in summer to stimulate growth, but it should be shaded from scorching sun, which can bleach the leaves. The soil should be allowed to dry between thorough waterings. Fertilizer can be applied monthly in spring and summer. Yucca needs infrequent repotting, only when the roots begin to grow through the drainage holes. It can be propagated from offsets and potted in an all-purpose soil mix.

Yucca is susceptible to aphids and scale insects.

━

Zebrina (ze-BRY-na)

Trailing green plant with fleshy stems to 3 feet in length. Leaves are pointed oval and 2 inches long. Small lilac, purple or rose flowers may bloom in spring or summer.

Selected species and varieties. *Z. pendula,* wandering Jew: has bright green leaves with broad, silvery lengthwise stripes. Undersides of leaves are flushed with purple. Flowers are deep pink.

Growing conditions. Wandering Jew needs bright light to produce its best leaf color. It thrives in average room temperature and medium humidity. The soil should be allowed to dry between waterings; overwatering can foster root rot. Fertilizer can be applied regularly in spring and summer. Dried leaves should be removed and stems should be pinched back to encourage full growth. Wandering Jew can be propagated from stem cuttings and repotted in an all-purpose soil mix.

Wandering Jew is susceptible to damage from scale insects, spider mites and whiteflies.

ZEBRINA PENDULA

FURTHER READING

American Horticultural Society, *Houseplants*. Mount Vernon, Virginia: American Horticultural Society, 1980.

Beckett, Kenneth A., *The RHS Encyclopedia of House Plants*. Topsfield, Massachusetts: Salem House, 1987.

Brookes, John, *The Indoor Garden Book*. New York: Crown, 1986.

Crockett, James Underwood, *Crockett's Indoor Garden*. Boston: Little, Brown, 1978.

Davidson, William, ed., *The Illustrated Encyclopedia of House Plants*. New York: Exeter Books, 1984.

Everett, T. H., *New York Botanical Garden Illustrated Encyclopedia of Horticulture*. New York: Garland, 1980.

Fitch, Charles Marden, *The Complete Book of Houseplants*. New York: Hawthorn Books, 1972.

Furata, Tokuji, *Interior Landscaping*. Reston, Virginia: Reston Publishing, 1983.

Halpin, Anne M., ed., *Rodale's Encyclopedia of Indoor Gardening*. Emmaus, Pennsylvania: Rodale Press, 1980.

Hay, Roy, and Patrick M. Synge, *The Color Dictionary of Flowers and Plants for Home and Garden*. New York: Crown, 1986.

Herwig, Rob, *How to Grow Healthy House Plants*. Tucson, Arizona: HP Books, 1979.

Langer, Richard W., *Grow It Indoors*. New York: Warner Books, 1975.

McDonald, Elvin, *The Hyponex Handbook of House Plants*. Copely, Ohio: Hyponex, 1975.

Oster, Maggie, ed., *The Green Pages*. New York: Ballantine Books, 1977.

Reader's Digest Editors, *Success with House Plants*. Pleasantville, New York: Reader's Digest Association, 1979.

Seddon, George, *Your Indoor Garden*. New York: Exeter Books, 1984.

Shakery, Karin, ed., *Ortho's Complete Guide to Successful Houseplants*. San Francisco: Ortho Books/Chevron Chemical Company, 1984.

Sunset Editors, *Houseplants*. Menlo Park, California: Lane Publishing, 1983.

Taylor, Norman, *Taylor's Guide to Houseplants*. Boston: Houghton Mifflin, 1987.

Wright, Michael, ed., *The Complete Indoor Gardener*. New York: Random House, 1979.

PICTURE CREDITS

The sources for the illustrations in this book are listed below. Cover photograph of blushing bromeliad and croton by Renée Comet. Watercolor paintings by Nicholas Fasciano and Yin Yi except pages 88, 89, 90, 91: Lorraine Moseley Epstein.

Frontispiece paintings listed by page number: 6: *Pineapple Bud,* c. 1939, by Georgia O'Keeffe, private collection, courtesy John Berggruen Gallery. 28: *Praying Mantis,* c. 19th century, Japanese Lacquer Writing Box, courtesy Metropolitan Museum of Art, New York. 60: *Begonias,* c. 1955, by Charles Sheeler, The Lane Collection, courtesy The Museum of Fine Arts, Boston.

Photographs in Chapters 1 through 3 by Renée Comet except where listed by page number: 12: Eric L. Heyer/Grant Heilman Photography. 30: Bob Grant. 44: Robert Lyons/Color Advantage. 66: Bob Grant.

Photographs in the Dictionary of Foliage Houseplants by Pamela Zilly, except where listed by page and numbered from top to bottom. Page 98, 1, 98, 2: Renée Comet. 98, 3: Robert Lyons/Color Advantage. 99, 1: Renée Comet. 99, 2: Pamela Harper. 99, 3: Connie Toops. 100, 1: Robert Lyons/Color Advantage. 100, 4: Derek Fell. 101, 1: Connie Toops. 101, 2: Derek Fell. 101, 3: Robert Lyons/Color Advantage. 102, 2, 103, 1: Connie Toops. 103, 2: Robert Lyons/Color Advantage. 104, 1, 104, 2: Connie Toops. 104, 3: Steven Still. 105, 2: Elvin McDonald. 106, 1: Connie Toops. 106, 2: Barry Runk/Grant Heilman Photography. 106, 4: Renée Comet. 107, 3: Bob Grant. 107, 4: Robert Lyons/Color Advantage. 108, 3: John Colwell/Grant Heilman Photography. 109, 1: Pamela Harper. 109, 2, 109, 3, 109, 4: Robert Lyons/Color Advantage. 110, 3, 110, 4: Pamela Harper. 111, 1: Renée Comet. 111, 2: Connie Toops. 111, 3, 112, 1: Robert Lyons/Color Advantage. 112, 2: Pamela Harper. 112, 3: Runk/Schoenberger/Grant Heilman Photography. 113, 2: Connie Toops. 113, 3: Pamela Harper. 113, 4: Connie Toops. 114, 1, 114, 2: Pamela Harper. 115, 1: Connie Toops. 116, 4, 117, 1: Robert Lyons/Color Advantage. 117, 2: Connie Toops. 118, 2: Robert Lyons/Color Advantage. 118, 3: Connie Toops. 119, 1: Robert Lyons/Color Advantage. 119, 2: Connie Toops. 119, 4: Robert Lyons/Color Advantage. 120, 3: Gillian Beckett. 121, 1: Robert Lyons/Color Advantage. 121, 2, 122, 1: Runk/Schoenberger/Grant Heilman Photography. 122, 2: Derek Fell. 122, 3: Pamela Harper. 122, 4: Connie Toops. 123, 1: Derek Fell. 125, 2: Robert Lyons/Color Advantage. 126, 1: Bob Grant. 126, 2: Robert Lyons/Color Advantage. 126, 3: Renée Comet. 127, 1: Anne Heimann. 127, 3, 127, 4: Connie Toops. 128, 3: Robert Lyons/Color Advantage. 129, 2: Barry Runk/Grant Heilman Photography. 129, 4, 130, 1: Robert Lyons/Color Advantage. 130, 2: Bruce Coleman. 130, 3: Robert Lyons/Color Advantage. 131, 1: Connie Toops. 131, 3: John J. Smith/Photo-Nats. 131, 4: Renée Comet. 132, 1: Robert Lyons/Color Advantage. 133, 1: Connie Toops. 133, 3: Robert Lyons/Color Advantage. 134, 1: Connie Toops.

ACKNOWLEDGMENTS

The index for this book was prepared by Lee McKee. The editors wish to thank David T. Scheid for allowing them to photograph plants belonging to the United States Botanic Garden, Washington, D.C. They also wish to thank: Bailey Hortorium, Cornell University, Ithaca, New York; Dr. Gail E. Beck, University of Wisconsin-Madison, Madison, Wisconsin; Deborah Bell, Smithsonian Institution, Washington, D.C.; Sarah Brash, Alexandria, Virginia; Ruth Burke, Alexandria, Virginia; Diane Cina, Horticulture Department, National Gallery of Art, Washington, D.C.; Karen Cogar, Alexandria, Virginia; Betsy Frankel, Alexandria, Virginia; Kenneth E. Hancock, Annandale, Virginia; Charles F. Heidgen, Shady Hill Gardens, Batavia, Illinois; Mary Kay Honeycutt, Crofton, Maryland; Dr. Dennis B. McConnell, University of Florida, Gainesville, Florida; Tovah Martin, Logee's Greenhouses, Danielson, Connecticut; Barbara Fox Mason, Alexandria, Virginia; Meredith Mercer, Alexandria, Virginia; Dan Nicolson, Smithsonian Institution, Washington, D.C.; Jayne E. Rohrich, Alexandria, Virginia; Jos and Eric Roozen, Roozen Nursery Inc., Fort Washington, Maryland; Roger Sanders, Fairchild Tropical Gardens, Miami, Florida; Candace H. Scott, College Park, Maryland; Lucille Shifrin, Gaithersburg, Maryland; Skip Shorb, American Plant Food Company, Inc., Bethesda, Maryland; Cynthia Spak, GreenSpace Unlimited, Washington, D.C.; Carol Stackhouse, Alexandria, Virginia; Nanci Stern, Fairfax, Virginia; Jo Thomson, Alexandria, Virginia; Karen Upton, Behnke Nurseries Company, Largo, Maryland; Arthur J. Wallace III, Parker Interior Plantscape, Scotch Plains, New Jersey; James Watson, Fairchild Tropical Gardens, Miami, Florida.

*Numerals in italics indicate an illustration
of the subject mentioned.*

REDEFINITION

Senior Editors	Anne Horan, Robert G. Mason
Design Director	Robert Barkin
Designer	Edwina Smith
Illustration	Nicholas Fasciano
Assistant Designers	Sue Pratt, Monique Strawderman
Picture Editor	Deborah Thornton
Production Editor	Anthony K. Pordes
Research	Mary Yee, Gail Prensky, Barbara B. Smith
Text Editor	Sharon Cygan
Writers	Mary B. Good, Gerald Jonas, Ann Reilly, David S. Thomson
Administrative Assistant	Margaret M. Higgins
Business Manager	Catherine M. Chase
PRESIDENT	Edward Brash

Time-Life Books Inc.
is a wholly owned subsidiary of

TIME INCORPORATED

FOUNDER	Henry R. Luce 1898-1967
Editor-in-Chief	Jason McManus
Chairman and Chief Executive Officer	J. Richard Munro
President and Chief Operating Officer	N. J. Nicholas Jr.
Editorial Director	Ray Cave
Executive Vice President, Books	Kelso F. Sutton
Vice President, Books	George Artandi

TIME-LIFE BOOKS INC.

EDITOR	George Constable
Executive Editor	Ellen Phillips
Director of Design	Louis Klein
Director of Editorial Resources	Phyllis K. Wise
Editorial Board	Russell B. Adams Jr., Dale M. Brown, Roberta Conlan, Thomas H. Flaherty, Lee Hassig, Donia Ann Steele, Rosalind Stubenberg, Henry Woodhead
Director of Photography and Research	John Conrad Weiser
Assistant Director of Editorial Resources	Elise Ritter Gibson
PRESIDENT	Christopher T. Linen
Chief Operating Officer	John M. Fahey Jr.
Senior Vice Presidents	Robert M. DeSena, James L. Mercer, Paul R. Stewart
Vice Presidents	Stephen L. Bair, Ralph J. Cuomo, Neal Goff, Stephen L. Goldstein, Juanita T. James, Hallett Johnson III, Carol Kaplan, Susan J. Maruyama, Robert H. Smith, Joseph J. Ward
Director of Production Services	Robert J. Passantino
	Editorial Operations
Copy Chief	Diane Ullius
Production	Celia Beattie
Library	Louise D. Forstall
Correspondents	Elisabeth Kraemer-Singh (Bonn), Maria Vincenza Aloisi (Paris), Ann Natanson (Rome)

THE CONSULTANTS

C. Colston Burrell is the general consultant for The Time-Life Gardener's Guide. He is Curator of Plant Collections at the Minnesota Landscape Arboretum, part of the University of Minnesota, and the author of publications about ferns and wildflowers.

Robert E. Lyons, consultant for *Foliage Houseplants,* is an associate professor of horticulture at Virginia Polytechnic Institute and State University in Blacksburg, Virginia, where he teaches courses in indoor plants and controlled plant environments. He is the author of numerous articles on flowering plants and houseplants.

Library of Congress Cataloging-in-Publication Data
Foliage houseplants.
    p. cm.—(The Time-Life gardener's guide)
    Bibliograpy: p.
    Includes index.
    1. House plants. 2. Foliage plants.
I. Time-Life Books.
SB419.F64 1988   635.9'65—dc19   88-20164 CIP
ISBN 0-8094-6620-1.
ISBN 0-8094-6621-X (lib. bdg.)

Time-Life Books Inc. offers a wide range of fine recordings, including a *Rock 'n' Roll Era* series. For subscription information, call 1-800-621-7026, or write Time-Life Music, P.O. Box C-32068, Richmond, Virginia 23261-2068.